AROUND THE VILLAGE GREEN

AROUND THE VILLAGE GREEN

The Heart-warming Memoir of a World War II Childhood

DOT MAY DUNN

ISIS

LARGE PRINT

Oxford

First published in Great Britain 2014
by
Orion
an imprint of Orion Publishing Group Ltd.

Published in Large Print 2014 by ISIS Publishing Ltd.,
7 Centremead, Osney Mead, Oxford OX2 0ES
by arrangement with
Orion Publishing Group Ltd.
an Hachette UK Company

CIP data is available for this title from the British Library

ISBN 978–1–4450–9968–2 (hb)
ISBN 978–1–4450–9969–9 (pb)

Printed and bound in Great Britain by
T. J. International Ltd., Padstow, Cornwall

To Alex, Joe, Fran and Nikiyah — the new generation.
May you never fight a war.

Acknowledgements

I would like to thank Amanda Harris, Orion Publisher, and Gillian Stern, my brilliant editor, who made it possible for me to find this book in a chaos of stories. Also to my brothers, Trev and Bill, who helped to remind me of those far-off days.

A note to the reader: while this book is about true events, which are in time and of essence, I would like to remind you that all of it has been filtered through 75 years of memory — think on!

Contents

1. Time Begins...1

2. The enemy is here.............................12
   October — December 1939

3. Who lives, who dies 23
   April — August 1940

4. The Military Camp.............................40
   September — December 1940

5. Changing times 60
   April — October 1941

6. They pass. They don't stay with us.............76
   May 1942

7. The silent war of waiting, waiting in hunger....86
   October 1942 — January 1943

8. The Yanks are coming.........................102
   March — July 1943

9. They came and they were like us, but they
   went, to where we knew not...................118
   September 1943 — March 1944

10. We know the face of one who died 131
    June 1944

11. A thousand rats to die 144
    September 1944

12. The enemy, my friend 167
    October — December 1944

13. The Last of the Enemy 186
    January — February 1945

14. A few return, too few 203
    March — May 1945

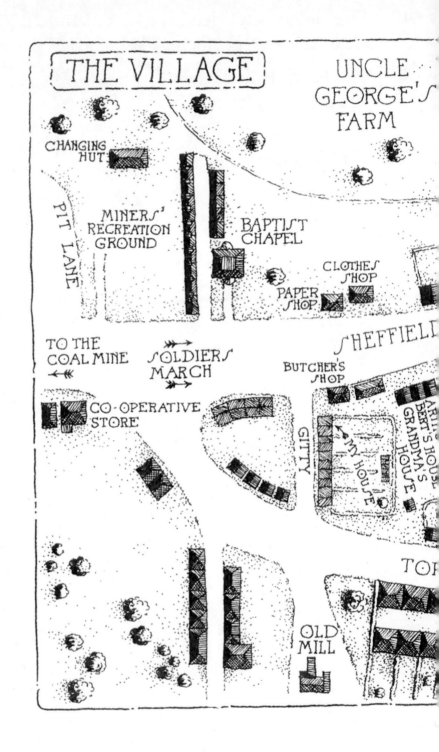

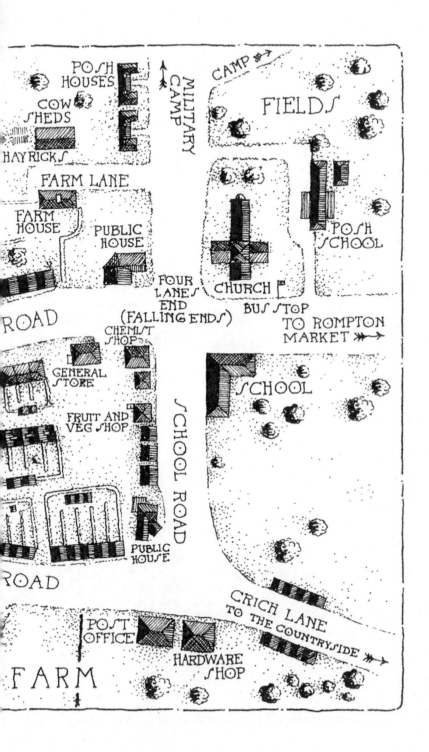

THE HOUSE

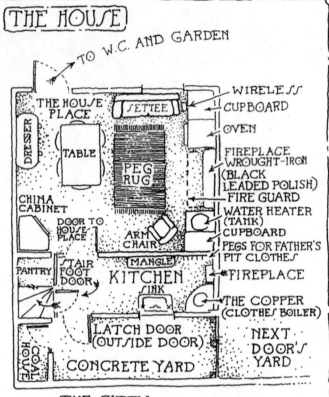

TO W.C. AND GARDEN

WIRELESS

CUPBOARD

OVEN

FIREPLACE WROUGHT-IRON (BLACK LEADED POLISH)

FIRE GUARD

WATER HEATER (TANK)

CUPBOARD

PEGS FOR FATHER'S PIT CLOTHES

FIREPLACE

THE COPPER (CLOTHES BOILER)

THE HOUSE PLACE

SETTEE

DRESSER

TABLE

PEG RUG

CHINA CABINET

DOOR TO HOUSE PLACE

ARM CHAIR

MANGLE

KITCHEN

STAIR FOOT DOOR

PANTRY

SINK

LATCH DOOR (OUTSIDE DOOR)

NEXT DOOR'S YARD

COAL HOUSE

CONCRETE YARD

THE GITTY

1ST FLOOR

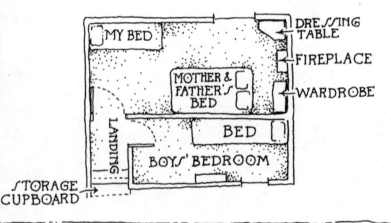

MY BED

DRESSING TABLE

FIREPLACE

WARDROBE

MOTHER & FATHER'S BED

BED

LANDING

BOYS' BEDROOM

STORAGE CUPBOARD

CHAPTER
ONE

Time begins

Father swings me on to the window ledge.

"Stay here for a moment, you two. Got to talk to the men about poor old Ken."

Jack and I kick our legs against the wall. Something bad has happened at the mine and Father needs to do his Union work, in the pub. My brother doesn't mind. Anything to put off going to Chapel. He is six and has to go to Sunday school. I am still too young.

The window opens and two glasses of lemonade appear. We can hear Father talking to the other miners.

"Look, we can't just sit around doing nothing. This is the second fall we've had recently. Ken was killed." There is a low mumble of voices and then Father's voice sounds even louder. "No. It's no good just talking. Them pit owners don't care at all. We could all die as far as they're concerned. There are hundreds unemployed out there. They can replace us in a flash."

My lemonade feels very cold. I don't like to hear Father talking about dying. Mother keeps saying how dangerous his work is, pleading with him to get another sort of job. "What other job, Nellie?" he asks her.

Voices rise. Father's voice rings out:

"It's no good just having a collection at the pit. We've got to get some proper compensation for them. Two men have lost their lives. We've got to get a committee together and write down what we want. It could be any one of us next. The pit isn't safe and the owners won't care if a whole face falls in. But they'll take notice if we all stand behind what we say, let them know that we will stand together."

"They won't listen to us, Joe, and you know it." I recognise my Uncle Arthur's voice.

Father's voice is sharp. "They will if we stand together. Let them know that we are together."

"You talking about a strike there, Joe?"

The window slams.

Now we are walking to Grandma Compton. Jack has to go to Chapel with my aunts. I am sitting atop Father's left shoulder. His coal-blue-stained hands pull my coat firmly down over my legs.

"Goodness, you're cold, Dolly!"

He shifts me close to his head and his hat tips to a jaunty angle. As he fixes it back down, he calls out:

"Jack, you wait for us now. Don't go rushing off."

We are outside the chemist, where an old man is sitting on a wooden bench. Father stops beside him. One trouser leg is tied up and he has to use a heavy crooked stick to walk. Mother says he lost his leg in France. I don't know where France is or how he lost it in France, but Mother says I must not ask him.

"Hear there's been another fall then, Joe." The old man's voice is croaky. I think he lives on that bench.

"Aye, Stan, and not much we can do about it."

"Don't want another strike. The last one did us no good: just got a gun turned on us, and half the pits shut." He turns his eyes to where the two roads in the village cross, and both men look at the spot. "Would have shot you too if you'd gone on. We'll all be dead soon anyway. No food."

Now I am frightened and clutch Father's head.

"Better get moving, Stan. This littlun's cold."

The church clock strikes. We pass the houses with doors right next to the pavement. A man steps out of the last house and I see two small boys in the doorway. Their faces are white, they are thin and dirty, and both of them are wearing torn jumpers — no trousers or shoes. They are like ghosts. Behind them the entrance to the house is black and I can smell something horrible coming from it. Everything about the man is grey — his coat, his trousers, his cap, even his face. As he turns, he almost bumps into Father. He steps backwards, makes a wide circle around us and touching the peak of his cap, looks down at the ground.

"Mr Compton."

Father nods his head. He looks back at the man's emaciated children and mumbles, "Wonder when they last ate."

Unsteadily, the man crosses the road and turns into the door of the pub.

"Poor bugger. Hope somebody buys him a pint," Father says.

Now we walk by a row of houses, which are set back from the road. Each one stands at the end of its own

3

long narrow garden, separated from the pavement by a low, brick wall. Jack is nowhere in sight. As usual he has made a run for it.

The door to one of the houses opens. My grandma steps out.

"You shouldn't come out in the cold, Mother."

Although Father chastises her, his voice is gentle. Grandma stands before us, her face turned upwards. She smells of cooking — newly baked bread and sweet almond cake. Her eyes smile, but only one side of her face can. She pulls at her shawl to hide the large scar that runs up part of her cheek.

"Saw Father up the pub."

"Just having a little drink before his dinner," says Grandma, looking at him hard.

She reaches up to take my hand. "Look how cold this little girl is! Have you had them up the pub again, Joe? Nellie will kill you."

"I had to do some Union work; I knew the blokes would be in there," says Father.

Father calls for Jack as he strides towards Grandma's door, swishing the curtain aside. Aunt Betty, Father's youngest sister, narrowly avoids us. The fox fur, bouncing on her shoulders, smells of rosewater.

"Are you in a rush, Betty?" asks Father.

The curtain has knocked my hat sideways, and it hangs down my back on its elastic string. Father swings me over his head and sits me on the large table in the middle of the room.

The blast of warm air, which is filled with the delicious smell of cooking, almost takes my breath

4

away. I know this house so well. Large pieces of dark brown furniture fight for space with all the people who live here — my grandparents, my aunts and my uncles. My favourite things are the grandfather clock, the lace doilies, the frills and pom-poms on the mantelpiece and the yellow canary in his cage.

Another one of my aunts comes through the curtain at the far end of the room and now I am the centre of attention. Usually I have to stand in the middle of the table, while Aunt Betty and Aunt Flo curl and decorate my hair. They both work at a large house on the edge of the village and collect ribbons and lace from the daughters of the house. As I am the only girl in the family, they use me as a model for the latest fashion in hair. Mother is rarely pleased with their attempts and as soon as I get home, I have to stand still while my plaits are returned. But there is to be no hairdressing for me today.

"Come along, Flo, or we will be late for the service," calls Aunt Betty.

"Can Jack go up with you?" Father asks.

Jack pulls a gruesome face.

"Hurry up then, Jack. Go and have a tiddle before we leave." Aunt Betty stops in front of the mirror to adjust her hat.

Uncle Arthur and Uncle Jim are back from the pub. They sit by the fire, their white-sleeved shirts rolled up to the elbow.

"Shut that door properly, Joe. It's enough to freeze the place with it open," says Uncle Jim.

5

"No Chapel for you then, Jim?" Father asks as he closes the door.

Uncle Jim looks at Father over his paper. "Don't see you rushing up there, Joe. Won't Nellie let you go? Oh, I forgot. Your sabbath is Saturday, isn't it?"

Father steps forward, but Grandma is there before him.

"That will do, Jim. Mind your mouth while you are in this house."

"Made it this far did you, Joe?" asks Uncle Arthur, an ugly sound in his voice. "You want to watch him, Jim, agitating in the pub earlier. Quite the revolutionary he is. He'll have us all on strike, or on the gallows, depending which comes first."

"Better to die with red blood in your veins than with a yellow streak down your back." Father says quietly as he picks me up from the table.

Uncle Arthur is now standing by the door, his face red and angry.

"Arthur, get out of the way and let them leave. I don't know what has got into you all." Grandma, no longer pink and soft, moves towards the door.

Adjusting fox furs, the partridge feathers standing high on their hats, my two aunts take Jack's hands and, in a column, in silence, squeeze past Arthur.

"Anyway," continues Uncle Arthur, "soon you won't have to worry about getting us lot work. Chancellor Hitler will be over shortly."

"Not if we can do anything about it: he won't be coming to our country," says Father.

Grandma pushes herself between her sons. She pushes a pudding basin into my father's arms, our Sunday evening pie.

"Haven't we had enough with war? The last one did us no good. Or have you lot forgotten how much we lost?" Grandma's face crumbles. "Go on home, Joe," she says softly.

"Say one for me," Father calls out as Jack is propelled down the road to Chapel.

Defying the brisk wind and slate-grey sky, I hang on to the back of my father's hair as we walk home, back around the village green. We turn down the gitty, a narrow muddy path leads to our back door. I want to see my baby brother, Bob. He always saves his biggest smiles for me, his yellow curls bouncing all over his head as he waves his little fists around.

Mother stays at home on Sunday mornings. She cooks what Father calls his best meal of the week, his "roast Sunday dinner". When my aunts bring Jack back after Sunday school, they don't come in because they are cross with Mother for never going to Chapel.

As I pull back the dark green velvety curtain it ripples over the doorway. Through this curtain is our house-place. An open fire is burning in a shining wrought-iron fireplace, polished to brightness with black-lead polish.

"Can I sit on the mat and do some colouring before Jack comes home?" I call out.

Mother comes in, holding Bob, who wiggles his fat arms out at me. She has her busy face on, her blue-grey eyes drawn together in a frown. Her smiling, pretty face, the one I have seen in the picture on our living-room wall, is not the one I see now, or very often. Her hair is pulled back from her face, tucked over and under a band, and I can smell soap as she bends over to take off my coat.

"Yes, but don't get your pencils everywhere. I'm in the middle of cooking."

My feet press down pieces of material as I walk across the mat to get my pencils. I love the new pegged rug — put together by Mother and Grandma from Grandma's old winter coat, some of Father's old trousers, someone's old jacket and other clothes. My feet leave a pathway through the rug. Like footprints in the snow, they remain after I have passed. I forget about my colouring as I play my favourite game of remembering which piece of clothing the strips in the rug are from. I lie down, face into it. The warmth of the fire makes me feel drowsy.

Father reaches over the fire to the mantelpiece and lifts down his pipe. The business of the moment begins. Blowing into the stem of the pipe, he looks into its bowl, blows again and then, leaning over the metal fireguard, taps it on a firebrick. Mother passes him the *Sunday Express*, and sitting back in his chair, he begins the process of lighting the pipe.

"Our Arthur is a silly bugger, you know. Says Hitler and all the Germans will be over here in six months. Says a war will do our country good. Says we need the Germans to get us going again."

8

Father's words come in short bursts as he sucks a flame through the tobacco in his pipe and gets the smoke billowing from his mouth.

Mother leans over the fireguard and, using a large piece of sacking to protect her hands, opens the door of the oven. Steam tumbles out, and the smell and hissing sound of cooking meat fill the air. Her face is red and her voice sharp as she looks across to Father.

"I don't want them to come for any reason. I don't think they will do us any good." She points towards the newspaper. "Doesn't look as though they are doing other places much good."

"I was just saying what that daft brother of mine said. I don't want them here, telling us what to do, and if they try to come we'll give 'em a bloody nose. That smells good, Nellie."

"Um!" she says as she starts to rearrange potatoes around it. "Went up Rompton market yesterday. Quite a battle it was, but I managed to get a small piece of beef."

"Put some lard on it so that I can have some dripping on toast next week. We won't let 'em in — don't you start fretting. People have tried to take us over but we don't let them. We fight 'em."

Mother lowers a large saucepan on to the fire, full of potatoes and turnip. There's enough in there to last us for a couple of days.

"But, Joe, wars are not good. Men die. Look what happened in the last one. The village is full of men who came back injured. You might have to go away and fight."

Having made several efforts to start reading his paper, Father now folds it and looks at her.

"I don't think I'd be called up. We were talking about this in the pit canteen the other day. The men think that there'll be reserved occupations as at the end of the last war. Us face workers will be in that. Always need coal."

"One good thing I read in a magazine across at the paper shop."

"Did you buy a magazine, Nellie?" Father butts in.

"Don't panic, Joe: I just read it on a stand. Anyway, it said that if there were another war they'd probably start rationing right at the beginning. Last time so much food was wasted by big hotels and clubs and things at the beginning of the war while the rest of us were starving."

"Could do with some rationing now," says Father, "to spread the food out a bit. We saw those kids who live down from Mother's. They looked as though they hadn't had a good meal in months."

The curtain to the houseplace shivers.

"Close the door, Jack! There's enough draught to cut your legs off. You'll freeze the dinner," shouts Mother.

Jack slams the door shut.

"And put that curtain right," she adds.

Jack throws himself on the settee with a loud crash.

"That's done for the week, then," he says grimly.

"Joe, pick that baby up, will you?" says Mother as she lifts the meat from the oven.

Bob squeals with delight as Father throws him in the air.

"Come on, lad. Let's see if we can find something worth listening to on this wireless."

The whistling sounds as BBC is located and the voice of Sunday dinnertime rings out: "It's that man again, it's that man again. Tommy Handley is here." Father sings as he carves our little joint of meat, and we join in with "We'll get by".

"Get yourselves to the table," says Father. His voice suddenly sounds sad. "Let's remember poor Ken and then let us be thankful for our lives and this food."

CHAPTER
TWO

The enemy is here

October — December 1939

The village has been quiet for days. Adults meet in huddles and Father comes home from work with an unsmiling face. I stay close to Mother, whenever possible hanging on tightly to her dress. When we go to bed, Jack tells me that his teacher says that we are going to fight the Germans. We aren't sure what that means, but think it might have something to do with the stern man on the wireless who said that we were "at war with Germany". When he said that, Mother cried out and Father pulled her to him, and they sat huddled together for a very long time. Now as Jack and I lie in bed talking, he says soldiers from our country will fight soldiers from their country, but we don't know when and where they are going to do this.

The autumn sunshine warms people up. We talk to people we have never spoken to before. A woman, whom I had never even seen until this moment, talks to Mother when we are waiting to be served in the Co-operative store.

"I don't know how you are going to manage with little ones, missus. Poor things — goodness knows what will happen to them."

She makes me feel frightened and I hang on to Mother's dress so tightly that I nearly trip her over; the only reassurance I get is a clip round the ear.

Jack finds out as much as he can at school and I try to listen to the wireless or to Mother's conversations in the shops, and when he comes home we sneak off and tell each other what have uncovered. We still don't know where the Germans are, or what they look like. Are they nearby? Do they look the same as us? From what he hears at school, Jack thinks that they are very dangerous and that they could be close by.

Arthur and Bert come back with Jack to play in our garden. They are our best friends and although they look completely different, they are twins. Our mother is friends with their mother. Albert, whom we call Bert, has a mop of brown hair and his eyes always seem to be half closed. Mother says this is because he has a squint but Jack says it is because his face is fat. Arthur, his older brother by ten minutes, has the same colour hair but it is much shorter on the top. He is always looking out for Bert and is quiet, the opposite to his twin, who doesn't stop talking.

We come to the unanimous decision that we have to be on the lookout for the Germans in the village.

A shop selling clothes has opened across the road from where we live. Grandfather Compton's butcher shop used to be there — his old slaughterhouse lies just behind our house, the long metal hooks and ropes still hanging inside — but that was knocked down and now a brand-new shop has opened. It is next to the paper shop and every time we go by, Mother looks into the window, sighing softly at the frocks on the mannequins and the blouses and cardigans laid out beneath them. One morning, she surrenders to the call and pushes open the door, shoving me into the shop before her. A warm, scented smell hits me. There is a lady putting dresses on hangers and placing them on a wooden rack. She is much taller than Mother and has pale yellow curls piled on the top of her head in a way that I have never seen before. Her dress has bright red poppies on it and her very high-heeled shoes are the same colour red. She turns and looks at us as we stand on the bristly mat.

"Can I help you, madam?"

The voice seems to come from very far away. She walks towards us, her hands held together in front of her. She smiles at Mother and makes a funny noise at Bob.

"Just having a look at what you've got," Mother says.

She heads towards the wooden rack and I am left standing on the mat. The lady bends down to me and I have to do a wide circuit of the shop to get to Mother's side. I catch hold of a piece of her skirt and hang on tight.

"You are lucky to have such fine children. How are you going to manage with a war on?" she asks Mother.

"Like everyone else, I suppose," Mother replies.

"I don't have any children." The woman smiles at me as she speaks.

"Then you're lucky." Mother glowers down at me. Pulling her skirt out of my hand, she pushes me away from her. "Dorothy, will you let go of my skirt? I can't move with you hanging on."

The tall lady steps towards me and folding herself down, takes hold of the ribbon at the end of one of my plaits. She has large red lips and blue all around her eyes.

"Yes, I would like to have a little girl like you. Maybe your mother will sell you to me for half a crown. You could come and live with me in my nice house and you wouldn't have to be bothered by that brother of yours. Will you sell her to me, Mother?"

I can't move, as she is still holding my hair. I can only look at the blue powder around her eyes. Turning from the wooden rack, Mother puts her hand on my head.

"No, I can't sell her today. I need her at home. And anyway, she's a lot of trouble."

Mother's voice holds laughter but I spring back. I want to be as close as I can so that I can grab her should she change her mind.

"Don't tread on my shoes," Mother says as she pushes me back towards the woman.

Once again I stand in the middle of the linoleum floor and the woman rises, putting her hand on my head. Without looking at me, she says in a very quiet voice, "Oh, I could pinch you."

At school Jack has been told that because of the war children all over the world are losing their mothers and fathers. They are wandering around alone, or have had to leave their homes and go and live with strangers. Now I think that the war is here in the shop, and that I am going to have to leave my home and come across the road and live with this red and blue tall lady. I tell myself to remember what she looks like and how she speaks, and which shop it is exactly, so that Jack and Arthur and Bert and our other friends, George, Harry and Mike, will know where to rescue me from if I am not at home when they come back from school one afternoon. George might not be any good, though, as he has no time for little girls and is always tutting at me when Jack brings me along to play.

At home I try to tell Jack about the lady in the shop as soon as he comes through the door, but he pulls a "don't speak now" face and, nodding towards the door, shouts:

"I'm going down to the lavatory, Mother."

"I'm going down to the lavatory, Mother," I echo.

The lavatory, at the end of the garden, stands in semi-darkness. Skeletons of daddy-long-legs dangle on spiders' webs above us and squares of old newspaper hang on a piece of string. This is our place for secrets. I tell Jack what happened in the clothes shop and as he stands using the lavatory, he hisses through the side of his mouth:

"That shop must be the centre of German intelligence in our village. They must buy and sell children and send them to live with other people."

There are lots of children in our village and Jack decides we need to protect them — and us. When we are next together, the twins, Mike, George, Harry, Jack and I vote that we should gather evidence as soon as we can. I am told to look out for any signs of other children going in but not coming out of the shop, while the others are at school.

And so it is that the seven of us find ourselves outside the clothes shop early on Saturday afternoon. Harry takes charge, as usual.

"Keep a lookout while we get around the back," he orders.

Bert is pushed to the middle of the pavement as lookout. The rest of us press ourselves against the side of the shop and make our way slowly round to the back. We are in for a shock, as we discover that the back of the shop is held up on stilts and that underneath are loads of boards — with writing on them that no one can read — and boxes of all shapes and sizes, as well as long thin strips of coloured paper. I sniff.

"Everything smells of the lady from the shop," I tell the others. I am, after all, the only one who has been inside it.

"Don't touch anything! There might be a bomb," commands Harry, who is now in junior school and has told us that the Germans might drop bombs on us. Earlier that morning he had warned, "If we find anything unusual, we mustn't touch it and we must tell our parents."

We can't decide if the things under the shop are unusual enough to tell our parents about. Harry decides we need more "evidence" and says we should watch the shop from the safety of Bert and Arthur's front garden. I don't think this will get us very far, but as usual Harry tells me that I am only a girl, and don't understand about spying. I say that he should remember that I am the one who has done *all* the spying and stomp off home.

The next Saturday, having planned to be braver, we huddle together under the back of the shop, away from the wind. Bert, who is again acting as watchout, gets very cold standing on the pavement and comes round to the back.

"I'm freezing," he shouts and throws himself under the shop on to a bundle of brown paper. Boxes begin to slide, tumbling one after another, and as I put up my arm to stop them hitting me, a hand with long white fingers comes towards me. Bert screams at the top of his voice:

"A body! There's a body!"

The hand, along with its arm, rises into the air. We turn and run, and we don't stop running until we reach the other end of the village. Bert and I are some way behind the others before we reach the entrance to the recreation ground. We charge down the path and into the small covered changing area. Leaning on the wall of the shelter, we regain our breath.

"It was a body," gasps George.

"A dead one?" I ask.

The team nod yes.

"What do we do now?" asks Mike. He has gone very white. His father was killed down the mine, his body broken.

"Tell a policeman," says Jack.

Arthur has other ideas.

18

"We could go back and look for the rest of the body."

"No way!" we yell.

"Our cousin Charlie could do it. He wears long trousers," Arthur tells us.

That clinches it. We agree to the twins asking their cousin to find the rest of the body. Arthur and Bert promise to let us know when Charlie has completed his grizzly task.

Jack and I wait anxiously. Two days later we are out playing when a thunderous voice roars down the garden.

"Jack, Dorothy, come into the house now!"

This is a voice to be responded to at once. Mother, who is standing by the door, wipes her hands on her apron front, startled.

"What's happened, Joe? What's happened?"

Not replying to her, Father descends on us.

"So what have you two got to say for yourselves?"

At that moment we can't think of a thing that we want to say about anything, and Jack steps back a little way.

"Stand still when I'm talking to you," Father roars. "Constable White has been to see Mr Baker. He said that Albert and Arthur reported a dead body under the clothes shop. He tells me you two were implicated in this."

I don't know what "implicated" means, but the thought of the dead body, the policeman and being in trouble makes me shrink, and tears come into my eyes. Raising the edge of the tablecloth, Father sits me on the edge of the table. His voice is quieter but still very stern.

"I know you were only playing, but don't play there again. The boxes were only clothes boxes and the arm was a model. It was made of papier mâché. You shouldn't be playing with things that don't belong to you." He draws in a deep breath. "But worst of all, your silly behaviour set off a rumour going around the village that these people are not like us. The man and lady who own the shop are nice people who have come from down south to sell clothes in our village. Sometimes you meet people who look different, talk differently and do different jobs. You can't just start talking about them and telling other people tales about them. You will make people start to doubt them, and soon the whole village will turn against them, especially in these dangerous times."

I have seen newsreels at the cinema in which people had all their belongings thrown into the street where bonfires were made of them. At this moment all the horrible things in the films become real and frightening. I want to tell Father that I mustn't be sold to the lady at the shop, or to anyone else. Neither should Jack or Bob, or any of the children in the village. I don't want all my things to be taken out of our house and set on fire. I don't want Germans to drop bombs on us. I want to stay in my home and I want things to be as they always are. I want to tell my parents that I will always be good. But I can't seem to get the words together, so I sit and cry.

★ ★ ★

We are back outside the shop the next Saturday morning. Only this time, the seven of us, plus three big boys, are all dressed in our best coats, buttoned to the neck. All the boys have neatly combed hair. The three wearing long trousers are the boys caught behind the clothes shop last Sunday evening. They had been striking matches and lighting pieces of paper, and someone told Constable White that they were trying to burn down the shop. When he arrived, they told him that they were there looking for a body, which their cousins had found under the boxes. The policeman helped them search, and after Albert and Arthur had been interviewed and the policeman had been to see Father, it was decided that we needed to say sorry to the clothes shop owners.

Constable White arrives on his bicycle, his cloak thrown over his shoulder, to see that justice is done. He said that I didn't have to go in, as I am so young, but Father told me that if I was old enough to misbehave, I was old enough to say sorry. In my best red coat and beret, and wearing my black patent leather shoes, I climb the two steps to the entrance of the clothes shop. I am following Jack, and Bert is behind me, with the rest of the gang behind him. Our parents stand on the pavement and wait, along with a gathering crowd. I look back as I enter. Mother has her hand to her mouth, as she always does when she is anxious, and I feel bad that I have made her worry.

The shop is very full and seems much smaller than when I was last there. The policeman clicks the door closed and coughs. I am standing close to a rack of clothes and shrink back in the hope that I might hide; but to my horror the clothes move and the lady who asked to buy me is standing right in front of me. A man is standing beside her and for the moment she does not appear to see me.

"These children have come to apologise for messing with your shop," Constable White says in a loud voice. "One at a time, now."

Eyes turn to me. I open my mouth and as a squeaky little "sorry" comes out, the lady bends forward and pulls me to her side.

This is it, I tell myself. I'm sold.

The apologies go on. The man nods seriously to each of the boys in turn and then speaks to the policeman. The red-faced boys file out, but the lady still has her hand on my shoulder and I hope that Mother will notice that I have not come out. The lady places a hand on each side of my face and kissing the top of my head, she pushes a lollipop into my hand. I shoot out of the shop and as I look back I think how strange adults are.

The lollipop is too tempting to ignore but as I unwrap it, I panic. What if I eat it and then the lady says I now belong to her? I find Jack and show him the lollipop. He nods gravely and promises that he, Arthur, Bert, George, Harry and Mike will mount an immediate search if one day I am not at home when they get back from school.

"Don't worry, Dolly," he says. "Now, you'd better hand that over to me. I will get rid of it for you."

And with that he swiftly pops it in his mouth.

CHAPTER
THREE

Who lives, who dies

April — August 1940

Aunt Lily runs into our house. She is out of breath.

"There's been a fall at the pit."

Mother has been doing the high-up dusting. She comes down off the chair, dropping her duster, and starts for the door. My aunt puts out a hand to stop her.

"Stay here, Nellie. They're bringing him now."

Father comes home on a wooden board, carried by men from the pit. There is red all over his shirt and he doesn't talk, and I think he is going to die. I rush over to him but Mother says, in a voice that I know I must obey:

"Go out and play, Dorothy."

I go into the garden, just as Grandma Compton arrives. She dashes past me and as the door closes, I try to see through the window; but even stretching as high as I can on tiptoes, I can only see the bottom of the net curtain. Then I remember that Father put some of Grandfather's bricks by the shed, so I drag them round one by one until I have made some steps.

Father is sitting bent over, his head almost touching his knees. The bricks wobble as my heart nearly flies out of my body. He is covered in gashes. The first one starts at his right shoulder and runs all the way across his back. At the top it is almost as wide as his shoulder. There are three others underneath, each ending on the other side of his back. There is blood coming from all of them. Mother is standing by the table, a large jar of ointment in her hand. I can see her lips moving, but I can't hear what she is saying. It's like watching a film at the Electric Theatre when the sound doesn't work. Then Father cries out so loudly that I can hear his pain through the window. My whole body jumps and my pile of bricks collapses. I come crashing down on to the concrete.

The door opens and Mother is in the yard.

"Get in, get *in*. Can't you give me *one* moment of peace, Dorothy?"

I leap to my feet. My knees sting and my elbows hurt, but I don't cry because Father is dying. Inside I fight back my tears and sit on the floor with my back to the wall. At least I can watch and make sure he doesn't die without my knowing.

Father sits in the chair, his chest bound in strips of white linen torn from an old bed sheet. He is holding a cup of tea, which smells of whisky, and he tosses three aspirin into his mouth. Mother brings in a clean nightshirt and holds it open before him.

"Are you going to be able to wear this, Joe?" she asks.

He lifts a hand.

"Let me finish this drink first."

His voice is hoarse and broken and I go tight inside. Jack flings open the back door. When he sees Father, he looks around wildly.

"What's happened?"

Mother takes him into the kitchen. When he comes back into the houseplace, he is very quiet.

We sit down to eat Grandma Compton's meat and potato pie, though none of us are very hungry. She says she will be back in tomorrow. Father doesn't eat anything and Mother tells him he should go upstairs to bed.

"Goodnight, Daddy," I say, as he shuffles to his feet. "We hope you feel better tomorrow."

We watch Mother lead Father upstairs, candle in hand. When she returns, Jack jumps to his feet.

"Is he going to die?"

Bob starts to cry and Mother, her face red and tear-smudged, turns away.

"Get up to bed, get up to bed."

She swings her arms round and ducking under them, without having washed or cleaned our teeth, we go upstairs.

I lie in my little bed in the corner of the room. I can hear Father moving in the large bed, his voice mumbling to himself. Suddenly I hear, "You all right there, Dolly?"

I want to run over to him, but I don't. I lie stiff and still and whisper in a croaky voice, "Yes, Daddy. Are you?"

There is a moment's silence.

"Getting there, Dolly. Getting there."

Father doesn't die in the night. The next morning there are two men in grey suits downstairs. Father is sitting in his armchair, looking like a ghost: his skin is white and his eyes are black — not just black from coal dust, but black inside so that the blue no longer shines. One of the men holds a wooden board that has papers clipped to it. The papers have a crown printed at the top of each sheet. The man without the board shakes Father's hand. I creep over to the settee and make myself very small next to Jack. I am not going to be sent outside again. I want to know who these men are and why they have come and what is going to happen to my father.

"Surface injuries, was it, Mr Compton?"

Father looks up at the clipboard man.

"If that's what you want to call them, Frank."

Mother, who is giving Bob his breakfast, stands up as if to speak, but Father raises his eyebrows and she sits down again. The other man takes the clipboard and the only noise in the room is the sound of turning pages. Even Bob is silent.

"I see that you are a Miner's Union representative, Mr Compton."

"I am that."

The man looks back at the papers.

"Are you the Compton who's been agitating for health and safety procedures?"

Father makes his voice sound strong.

"Aye, Mr Armstrong, that's me: I've been fighting for the introduction of safety measures in the mines for years. Men have been dying like vermin. Did any die this time?"

Jack and I look at each other. I think of Mike and how his dad is already dead. Has another of our friends now got a dad who has died down the mine?

The man does not reply, but continues to look at his papers.

26

"We can't afford to lose manpower now, can we, Mr Compton?"

Smiling, he passes the clipboard back to the other man, who does not smile:

"We'll see you back on shift a week today, Mr Compton."

"I'll see you then, Frank," Father replies.

A week later, Father hurts too much to go back to the pit, so he stays at home for all of the next week. While Jack is at school, I sit very still on the peg rug, colouring or looking at my picture books but secretly making sure he isn't going to die. He spends most of the time sitting in his chair, reading his newspaper.

One morning, Grandfather Compton comes to see Father. He carries two red hens — one under each arm — and I am sent out into the yard. I am being good for Father but I go reluctantly. Grandfather does not come to our house very often. I start to pile up my bricks again but I am soon called back inside.

"Dolly, your grandfather thinks that there might be enough room at the bottom of our garden for these hens. Do you think we could look after them?"

"Where will they live?" I ask. "Will they just walk around the garden?"

"No, they'll have a shed to roost in and we'll build a pen for them to run and scratch in."

Grandfather, Father and I go back outside. Father walks slowly but is smiling for the first time since the coal fell on him. We have a toy shed which stands at the top of the garden and Father nods his head towards it.

"We're not going to build a shed. We'll use that one."

Jack comes through the gate and I rush towards him to tell him about the hens. His voice rises high as he follows Father's gaze.

"Do you mean our toy shed?"

Our toy shed is the one place that Jack and I — and sometimes Bob — have to ourselves. I have a doll's pram with a hood and one black doll and one pink doll. Jack has a wooden train painted in red and black, which he uses to pull a wooden carriage piled high with little bricks.

Grandfather has a brick in his hand and is driving a piece of wood into the ground. Mother and Bob are on the step, watching us.

"Are they going to take *our* shed?" Jack repeats, all wound up. He runs towards Grandfather.

Mother shouts: "Get out of the way, Jack, before you get hurt! Such a fuss over an old shed — you never use it nowadays. The hens will lay some eggs for us and help out with the rations."

I have heard Mother talking about rations when we are in the shops and this is something to do with the war. She spends a long time every day now looking in yellow, green and blue books and she is always searching for coupons to buy something with. She says that soon it will be very hard to buy what we like and we will only be allowed a few things to eat.

Now Mother is smiling as she watches Grandfather and Father. She does not smile very much and suddenly I think that it would be good to have the hens, as they will lay eggs for us and we will have food. Then

Mother won't have to give me to the lady in the clothes shop in exchange for rations.

The toy shed is carried to the bottom of the garden. Grandfather is very clever at making things and soon it has a new roof, a wire pen running down one side and a small round hole with a sliding door. He and Father lift it on to the bricks that have been my steps and with perches made of broom handles and a box of hay on the floor, the hen house is ready.

"Go and open the pen door, Dolly," says Grandfather.

I turn the wooden bar and swing the wire door open. In fly the two red hens, fussing, cackling and blowing out their feathers. I step back from their yellow claws.

"Are they both girls?"

Grandfather laughs. He has a sort of bubbly laugh that Mother says comes from too much Thin Twist.

"I hope so."

"What are their names?"

Grandfather laughs again and this time he almost chokes before he replies.

"I'm not sure, but I think they're Henrietta and Harriet."

Jack doesn't like this and even though I try to stick to Henrietta and Harriet, they soon become Henry and Harry. When Grandfather brings two more hens the next day, we call the one with a piece missing from her wattle Horace and the other, who is black and white, Matilda.

At least I've got one girl, I say to myself, as Bob and I look at them through the wire. Bob loves them, gurgling in hen talk as they strut around pecking at the ground. I am amazed when I see the eggs they lay and I love collecting them for our tea.

‎⋆ ⋆ ⋆

We save all the food scraps for our new animal family. Mother boils them and mixes them with cornmeal and the hens love to eat this. But a few weeks later, she announces:

"We won't be able to buy corn or cornmeal for much longer. I don't know what we will feed the hens on when we can't get any more."

Father, who is back at work, his big gashes getting better, looks at her over his pipe.

"I'd better have a word with Mother and see if she can fix it for us to go gleaning at harvest," he replies between puffs.

A few days later, Grandma Compton comes to take Jack and me to her sister's husband's farm so that we can talk to my uncle, whom we always call Uncle George. As soon as we turn into the yard, the geese come at us, hissing and honking, but Grandma is ready with her stick. She whacks them round the head and, cowards that they are, they soon turn around and waddle off. The whole place smells of cows and manure. As we pass the sharpening stone, we walk through the farmyard, past the barn where the cows stand, past the high hayricks, round the side of the house and into a small stone yard.

"I think I saw Uncle George milking the cows in the shed. Why don't you two go and ask him if you can watch?"

Jack runs ahead as Grandma keeps on to the house. I try to walk towards the cowshed, but my feet slip on the mossy slabs. I look around. Jack has disappeared

30

and I am alone. There is hay everywhere; its sweet smell fills the air. In the half-light I see a mountain of it rising high above me. I have to lean backwards, until I almost fall over, in order to see the top. I follow streaks of light that are coming through the roof of a barn. Hay is all around me and I feel as though I am sinking into it. I climb up some of the hay and sit down, hoping that Jack will come and find me.

Something moves by my foot. I fall back into the hay. Nothing happens, so with a fast-beating heart I part the hay. There, in a nest, are some tiny baby rats. I bend down to count them. *Seven!*

They have pink and grey bodies, little pink noses and the tiniest paws I have ever seen, and their eyes are closed. I sit down beside them.

"Hello, what are you doing here?" I ask them.

The little bodies wriggle against each other. I put my finger out and touch one of them. It is warm and soft.

"Dorothy, where *are* you?" Jack's voice comes ringing through the hay.

"Here," I answer, struggling to my feet.

"Come *on*! Uncle George is over here."

I look down at my babies.

"Be good. I'll be back soon," I whisper, full of love. I put the hay back over them as gently as I can and slide down to the ground.

After the light of the hayrick, it takes a bit of time for my eyes to see in the darkness of the cowshed. I have never been this close to cows before. They are like big, heavy monsters, their mouths moving slowly. They smell really bad and I want to go back to my sweet baby rats. When the cows see Jack and me, they all turn round and look at us with their big brown eyes. They moo and stamp and I move nearer to my brother.

"Steady, steady girl. Don't knock things over."

The cow nearest to us moves sideways and I see Uncle George. He is sitting on a stool and his head and shoulders are pushing hard into the side of a cow.

"Steady! Steady! Steady!"

He repeats the words as the cow tries to turn around to look at us.

"Who's there?"

His voice is stern and loud and he looks out under his knitted eyebrows.

"Is that young Jack? Come over here, my lad."

He puts his head back in the cow's side.

"And who's that with you?"

"It's Dorothy, Uncle George."

Jack pushes me and I stumble forward.

"My goodness, I didn't know she had grown so big." Uncle George's voice sounds all muffled beside the cow.

"We've come to ask if we can watch the milking," Jack says.

"Then you'd better come and look," says Uncle George.

Jack takes one step forward, but I am still unsure. There is a large silvery bucket under the cow and Uncle George, who is sitting on a stool, is holding two long pink tubes that hang from a sack under the cow. He squeezes and pulls on them, and each time he pulls, a jet of milk squirts into the bucket with a swishing sound.

"Come on, then," he says.

"Go on, Dot," hisses Jack.

32

As I step forward, a jet of warm milk hits me in the face. With a start I step backwards, gasping for breath, and as I wipe the milk from my eyes I can see Uncle George's shoulders shaking up and down with laughter.

"Open your mouth, Jack," Uncle George calls.

Jack gets his mouth wide open and a jet of milk shoots into it.

"Now you littlun, come on."

I am still not too sure, but I open my mouth as wide as I can and a warm, sweet jet fills my mouth, making me swallow hard. I close my mouth, thinking I might drown if I keep it open.

With all this noise, the cows have turned around to look at us again and they start mooing and stamping. Uncle George stops laughing.

"I think you'd better go and play in the hay until I've finished. Mind you don't get climbing too high."

We half walk, half run past the cows. As we reach the hayrick, Jack says in his bossy voice:

"I'm going to climb as high as I can. You have to stay below. Otherwise Uncle George will be cross."

For once I don't argue with him. As soon as he is out of sight, I search for my babies. It takes a bit of time, but I find them. I sit down in the hay beside them. I think that I must be like a monster to them, so I talk in a whisper, telling them that I am back to look after them. They lie curled around each other in their nest. One baby, who is bigger than the others, turns himself around and faces away from the others. I decide he must be a boy rat. I laugh as he rubs his small pink paws over his face and I put out a finger to stroke him. His teeny tiny paws come up and touch my finger.

I am watching the other babies, thinking about how Father might let me take them home so that I can look after them, when a voice behind me asks:

"What have you got there?"

I try to move away from the babies and my face burns red as I lie:

"Nothing."

Uncle George kicks the hay to one side. My babies squirm around and I fall down beside them. I cry out as I try to scoop them together.

"Leave them, leave them! They are my babies. I'm going to keep them."

But my small hands are not large enough and his large brown boots stamp the hay.

"You can't have them. They're rats. Vermin!"

I hit his boots with my fists.

"Don't, don't! You're a big bully. Stop!"

Without another word he swings me up under his arm and grabs a spade. The hay turns red.

"You're not having them, Dorothy. They're dead. I've killed them and I want no more crying and shouting from you."

He turns me upside down and marches out of the hayrick. I have to stop crying in order to start breathing again. When he places me on my feet, pain stabs my throat and chest, and I sob.

"Stop this noise, Dorothy! I've never heard anything like it. Rats have to die."

34

Now I can hear my grandmother running towards me. She lifts me in her arms and her face presses against my head.

"What on earth has happened, George?" she asks.

"I just killed some vermin. What a to-do!"

Grandma takes me inside to her sister, and after a glass of milk and a bit of bread, I calm down enough to be able to go home.

I dream about my babies. Their blood is mixed with the blood from Father's cuts and the coal from the mine. I pray that my special baby ran away before the spade came down, but Jack says he didn't stand a chance. Father has heard what happened from Uncle George and asks me what I had been thinking. How would we give rats anything to eat, he asks, when we don't have enough food for ourselves and our hens? He tells me that I must say sorry to Uncle George for throwing such a silly temper tantrum. I don't take much notice of this. I can't imagine I will ever see Uncle George again.

The ash tree by the paper shop comes to life. Now the green branches hang almost to the pavement, heavy with yellow keys. The sky is blue in the morning, but by mid-afternoon the hot sun has bleached out the colour and only a yellow glare remains. The heat haze shimmers and, like a mirage on some distant desert, the pavement dances. The long school holiday starts, which means that at last my days are full of Jack, Harry, George, Arthur, Bert and Mike. We spend little time on

35

the streets, instead making our way to the fields and streams around the village.

We are sitting with our feet in a stream when a low, throbbing sound fills the still, hot air. We look around us and then we see something skim the top of the hills, its black form rising out of the sun, its sleek wings shining. The white whirl of a propeller is above us and the roar of an engine vibrates in the air. The aeroplane rises at a steep angle, passes over the village and is gone. For a few moments my feet remain in the water, weeds clinging to them, but then I am standing.

"Did you see that?" says Bert, his face shining with excitement.

We all look to the spot where the aeroplane disappeared, but it doesn't reappear. Then, as if a spell has been broken, we grab our shoes and run towards the village. People are standing on the streets, mesmerised, silent. There are no words to speak. Grandfather is standing at the end of his path. I stand by him, my feet still bare, my shoes in my hand. I watch the sky. Without looking at me, Grandfather puts a hand on my head and speaks to the heavens:

"God help us. What will come next?"

Grandfather is sure that the Spitfire — the first aeroplane to cross our skies — means danger. I try to tell this to the boys, but they are too busy playing planes — holding out their arms and zooming down the road, the ferocious heat forgotten.

As it gets near to harvest time, I am worried that Uncle George won't let us help with the gleaning. But when

Father tells us that we are on our way to the farm, I don't want to go in case I see Uncle George. I make myself be brave for the sake of our hens, as Jack has said it's the only way we can get food for them. It is very hot and even walking to the farm is difficult. The air around us is thick and heavy and still.

When we get there, I stay behind Father, hoping that no one will notice me as we go through the gate and into the fields. We have gone only a little way along the cobbled lane, which is now covered in straw, when the head of a large shire horse appears over the brow of the hill. He is coming towards us pulling a cart. I am so pleased to see him that I forget to be cross. He lowers his enormous head to have his nose stroked and I run forward.

"Top field, Joe," comes a voice from the horse. I look up. Sitting high upon horse carried cart, with a mountain of wheat stooks behind him, Uncle George towers over us. I feel my face turn red and I slide behind Father's legs. We set off to the top field, where I am soon picking up the heads of wheat that the reapers have missed.

Happy that Jack and I have a leather bag full to bursting and our hens will have food this winter, we go back to the farmyard. It is very busy, alive with noise and people and wheat. Smoke is pouring out of the chimney of a huge, black machine and the clang and whirl of the cogs make my ears hurt. The large wheel turns with the chug of the engine and a great big black belt moves forwards and forwards and forwards.

Bundles of wheat drop into a huge hole in the machine. There is chaff and straw everywhere — in the air, over the yard, over everyone's hair and clothes. There are men running backwards and forwards, throwing stooks of wheat on to the belt. There are men with their backs bent double, heavy sacks being lifted and carried into the barn. Darkness is falling and two storm lamps are making long, eerie shadows in the warm, dusty evening.

We sit by a flowerpot and eat warm bread and fresh milk. Uncle George is leaning against the wall by the back door. I try to make myself invisible.

"Been a good harvest," he tells my grandfather.

"Hum. Let's hope we're not feeding Germans by the end of the year." Grandfather strikes a match and puts the flame to his pipe.

There is silence for a moment. I look up at their faces. Uncle George's voice is sharp as he pushes himself from the wall.

"I'll burn the bloody lot, including the farm, if they come."

He is gone. Suddenly I am afraid, of something bigger than Uncle George. Mother has told me that the Germans are evil. I thought that the grown-ups would know what to do if they came, but Uncle George is going to burn the farm. Someone comes up behind me and sits down on the step, pushing a leg between me and the flowerpot. I am suddenly very tired and my body feels heavy.

"Want a drink of beer, young'un?"

With a start, I realise that I am leaning on Uncle George. I try to get up to run away, but I am too tired. A large hand lands on my head and ruffles my hair.

We are friends.

"Sorry," I murmur and sleep washes over me.

CHAPTER
FOUR

The Military Camp

September — December 1940

"Our Charlie says that there are some Germans in the village."

We manage to unscramble this information as the twins talk at once. Since Charlie and his friends nearly set fire to the clothes shop, we have been under strict instructions not to mix with older children. But Charlie is Arthur and Bert's cousin, so they are allowed to see him.

Jack and Mike, who are digging a shelter for the hens under their shed, stop mid-shovel and give the twins their full attention. My first half-term of school has ended and we are looking for adventures to fill our days. I am now almost five and a half and a fully fledged member of the team.

"Has he actually *seen* any Germans?" Jack sounds as though he doesn't believe the twins.

"No. But someone from his school said that there are German prisoners of war in a camp and that they live there now."

"Will your dad and the other soldiers have to fight them?" I ask. Arthur and Bert's father has stopped being a miner and has become a soldier. Our father is needed in the pit because he puts the props in and lays out the face, so he hasn't got any of the calling-up papers that the postman has been delivering around the village. He does have a war job to do, though: going round the village checking for strangers and making sure everyone has their curtains closed at blackout time. When he does this he wears an armband and a tin helmet with a big W on it that Mother keeps on top of the mangle. Jack and I are desperate to try it on but we aren't allowed to touch it.

"Our soldiers have gone. They went away on lorries ages ago," shouts Bert. He is missing his father and doesn't like to talk about it.

This is now a different story.

"We can ask our father if it's true," I tell the boys.

"No." Jack lowers his voice. "You know what he said about talking of things we know nothing about. I think we should find out more ourselves before we ask anyone else."

Looking back at the house to make sure no one is watching, we scoot behind the hen house and make our plans. The air raid shelter for the hens is forgotten.

After dinner, Jack asks Mother if we can go down to play in the fields. She spits on the bottom of the iron, waits for it to bubble and holds it over Father's boiled and dried white shirt. Tuesday is ironing day — three irons on the go — and that means Mother is hot and bothered. As usual, she answers a question with another question.

"Who's we?"

"Bert, Arthur, Mike, Harry and me," Jack says. My heart thuds.

"You're taking Dot with you," replies Mother. For once I am grateful for her rules.

The six of us meet on Bert and Arthur's front door steps. Mike's mother always thinks that he will die of starvation if he leaves the house without food, so he arrives armed with two slices of bread wrapped in newspaper and a bottle of water. Bert has snaffled a bottle of pop, but as this is a bit too heavy to carry, we sit on the step and drink it. The day is overcast but at least the rain has stopped. Taking large strides and an occasional skip, I keep in step with the boys. Turning left at the falling ends, the point at which the road out to the east and the road out to the west meet, we march down the hill and out of the village, a serious brigade of foot soldiers.

"Do you know where we go now?" asks Mike.

"Charlie said that the soldiers' camp is at the bottom of the hill on the right-hand side," says Bert. We continue to march in formation until Harry pushes Mike into a hedge and we all fall off the pavement. Passing the entrance to Uncle George's farmyard I stop — as always — and say a little prayer for my baby rats. When we reach the bottom of the hill, we come to an abrupt halt. We look to the right but can't see anything that isn't usually there.

"They must be hiding," I say. "Where do Germans hide?"

"My grandfather says that they hide in holes in the ground, and when you get near them they jump up and

42

shoot you." Mike uses the first two fingers of his right hand to show us how Germans shoot and a battle erupts, until Harry shouts from across the road:

"Come on! I think we go this way."

We follow him. After all, the Germans can't be underneath the main road: no one could dig holes in that road. I keep in step, smartly swinging my arms. Mike swings a bit too far and the bread shoots out of the paper that he has been clutching. We laugh, but Harry makes a loud hushing sound and we fall silent. I pick up a large piece of bread and walking on tiptoe, take it back to Mike. He puts it on the newspaper with the other pieces and makes a parcel that he pushes up his jumper. With our food supply safe, we set off again. The road takes a sharp turn and we nearly fall on top of each other as Jack stops in front of an enormous metal gate.

Its thick metal grids are topped with coils of barbed wire. Hardly breathing, we stop dead still and watch as something moves behind the gate. Between the cracks I can see a man in soldier's uniform. He has belts around his shoulders and on his head sits a white helmet with the letters "MP" on it. He is carrying a gun in one hand. I nearly jump out of my skin as the gates begin to rattle and the loudest bark I have ever heard rings out. At the same time a thunderous voice roars.

"Who goes there?"

I have played the game of shouting "Who goes there" a million times and I know that I must now either fall down or run away. But my legs won't move and as I stand rooted to the spot I watch in terror as the dog hits the gate. A hand pulls at my jumper.

"Run, Dot, run!"

Again the dog hits the gate and this time I run. Harry shouts something and I see the boys dive into the long grass at the side of the road. Bert goes down last, not quite making it into the grass. I can see his bottom sticking out, but before I can push it out of the way, a lorry comes around the corner.

"Hide!" screams Harry.

But it is too late. The lorry slows down and a soldier shakes his fist at me.

"Bloody kids! Get out of here and bugger off home."

When the lorry reaches the gates, the soldier with the dog swings them open, and as it passes through the angry soldier leans out and points back towards us. This time I don't need to be told: I turn and run.

Gasping for breath, we fall on to the grass at the top of the road.

"That was a close one," says Arthur, panting.

"My legs are covered in nettle stings," says Bert.

But no one takes any notice of him.

"Didn't see much, did we?" Mike grumbles.

"Do Germans speak like us?" I ask, thinking of the words slung at me out of the lorry window.

"Stupid!" snorts Harry. "They're English soldiers *guarding* the German prisoners. The Germans are in the camp behind the gates." He is standing on tiptoes, looking over the hawthorn hedge at the side of the road. "If we sneak up the back drive of that posh school, I bet we could get into the fields at the edge of the camp. We could get a better look at it from there."

We look at Harry in horror.

"It's easy," he says as he lifts his hand and raises his shoulders. "I've been up there scrumping with some of the lads — done it lots of times." Harry is four years older than us and has had lots of real adventures, without us.

Father has told us to stay away from the posh school. I start to remind Jack of this but Harry is pointing at me.

"*She* can't come."

That does it. But before I start up my protest Jack says quietly, "I can't go if she doesn't."

"And we *won't* go if Jack doesn't go," says Bert.

Harry looks at them. "All right, then. Suppose she's useful for fitting into small gaps," he says.

Having refreshed ourselves with a drink from Mike's bottle of water, we set off. The back drive to the school opens on to the road leading up to the village, and to our amazement it is wide open. As we pass through, we keep close to a privet hedge and I can hear the dry leaves crunching under my feet.

We skirt the house and the fruit trees where Harry and his friends have scrumped. His navigation seems to be good, because when we get to the end of the orchard there are open fields stretching before us. We tear across them and, for once, I manage to keep up, Bert puffing along behind me. As we reach the other side, we come face to face with a hedge. We stretch our heads back as far as they can go but still can't see beyond it.

"Right, clever clogs, how are we going to get past this?" Arthur sneers as he pushes Harry.

We are standing looking at the hedge, trying to work out what to do, when Mike calls, in the loudest whisper he can manage:

"Look! Posts! Barbed wire!"

Hardly able to contain his excitement, Harry shouts:

"It's the camp! It's the camp!" He lowers his voice. "I *told* you we'd find it. We've got to get through this hedge *now*."

Bert looks rather pale. All the sprinting has done him no good and he starts to wail.

"Let's rest for a minute," says Harry, now the undisputed commander of our expedition.

Throwing his arms above his head, Bert collapses on to the grass. A vote is taken and he is allowed to have a swallow of our precious water. Determined to prove to Harry that girls are great explorers, I crawl along the bottom of the hedge to see if I can find a way through. A bit further up I spot a small gap between two of the trunks of the bushes, where the branches haven't knitted together.

"Over here!" I shout.

Harry sneers as the boys examine the hole.

"That's not big enough. We'll never get Bert through that."

"We *will*!" I cry.

I push my head and shoulders into the gap, but that is as far as I get. There is a ripping sound and to my horror I see that my jumper is torn. A vision of my

46

mother's face comes before me and in a panic I try to back out. But I can't move.

"I _knew_ we shouldn't bring a girl. Something always happens to them," says Harry.

I hear Jack's voice close behind me. "Let me talk to her. You might frighten her," says Jack kindly. "Dot, can you crawl forward?"

"Only if you unhook me," I whisper over my shoulder.

Jack skilfully unhooks my jumper and I shoot through the gap.

"Come on, squeeze yourselves," I call, as I lie on the ground peering back through the hole.

Jack tries, but he can't get more than his head in.

"I'll come back," I decide.

But Harry's head is blocking the gap and his loud hissing whisper halts me.

"No! At least take a look at what's through there before you come back."

I smile to myself. Now who wishes they were a girl and could squeeze through?

"OK." Rising up on to my knees, I take stock of where I am. Long, very green grass spreads out before me and a little way off stands a magnificent horse chestnut tree. Joy! Where there is a horse chestnut tree, there are conkers, and I can see hundreds of untouched precious jewels, glistening in the damp leaves. There are even more trees beyond this one. I didn't think a prisoner-of-war camp would be such an Aladdin's cave.

"What's there? What can you see?" demands Harry.

"There are some _fantastic_ conker trees," I call.

For a moment the Germans are forgotten. Yesterday we were searching the village for conkers, the boys eager to stock up for the long battle season ahead.

Jack's voice is trembling with excitement. "How many are there? Can you get some and pass them through?"

But Harry is not having it. "Never mind the conkers. Where's the camp?"

I come back to reality and tell them what I can see: large grey metal posts, line after line of wire and a road running around outside the posts. It is silent and still, and no one is in sight.

"Walk a bit further along the hedge and see if we can get through," commands Harry.

Now for the first time I realise that I am alone on the camp side of the hedge.

"I'm scared," I say.

"We'll walk along beside you. You'll be able to see us through the hedge," says Arthur, kindly.

I run along my side of the hedge, trying to keep sight of the boys. At times it is very thick and I lose them. Several times they think they have found a place to get through, but it is never large enough either for them to crawl through to my side or for me to get back to theirs.

My legs are beginning to feel shaky and I need to go to the toilet.

"Bob down and do it in the grass," says Jack.

Because I am walking close to the hedge and in a small ditch, the grass and nettles are almost to my shoulders, but before I can do anything an urgent call comes from the far side of the hedge.

"Down! Down! Get down!"

Without a second thought I am down on my face. I can hear my own heart beating and nothing else, so after a few seconds I lift my head and peer through the grass. I am just about to move when I hear the loud crunch, crunch, of heavy boots as they hit the concrete and gravel road. I drop down, hardly daring to breathe. The crunching gets louder and louder until it comes to an abrupt stop.

"Sit, damn you. Why are you being so skittish this afternoon?"

I brace myself, face pushed into the grass, waiting for a hand to grab me, but nothing happens except for a warm soft feeling spreading up my front. I am going to cry, but before I can draw breath, the voice above me speaks again:

"All right, Billie?"

I hear the crunch of boots again and another voice replies:

"Suppose so, but I'd be better if I were on a football pitch."

"Or on the missus," laughs the first voice.

Both men roar. Then I hear heavy breathing and as I look to see where it's coming from, I realise that I am looking into the face of the most enormous dog I have ever seen. Black hairs stick out of its muzzle, its ears are standing up high and stiff, and it is barking so loudly that I think I will be sick with fright. Its sharp brown eyes watch me as it raises one side of its top lip to reveal white fangs that look as long as my hands. It stops barking and growls, its horrible breath wafting over me.

49

"Sit when I tell you, you bloody thing," says one of the men and I hear the rattle of a chain.

The dog has stretched itself in order to sniff me and now, with a turn and another sharp yank, it returns to his master's side, keeping its beady eyes on me while raising its hackles and baring its teeth every few seconds. The smell of cigarette smoke fills the air and after a moment one of the boots grinds out a butt end, which a hand then picks up and throws in my direction. The dog stands and moves towards me, and the soldier pulls on the chain.

"What's *wrong* with you this afternoon? He's been so unsettled these past few days," he says as he tightens the chain around his hand.

"Is he young?" asks the other man.

"Not had him long. I'm training him in. But the bugger will have to learn fast, like the rest of us," he replies as he pulls the dog to his heel.

"I think it's the weather. Looks as though we are going to have a storm. They're all barking and going at it over there."

The two men walk away. Now I let myself burst into tears. Shaking from head to foot, I cry into the grass. I am terrified that the dog will come back for me to get his revenge. I try to stand and walk, but my legs are shaky and I feel sick, and I fall back into the grass. Crying seems to be the only thing that I can do. It is only when I take a big breath between sobs that I hear a voice coming from the other side of the hedge.

"Dot! *Dot!* Is that you?"

I am so relieved to hear Harry's voice that I cry even harder.

"Jack! She's further up, by the camp."

A loud shushing sound echoes around me. All of a sudden, a figure looms through the dark and, terrified it is the dog, I try to run. I am about to scream, when a soft voice says:

"Dot, Dot, is that you?"

It is Bert. Bert — who whimpers his way out of everything, who can't climb, can't run, can't seem to do anything much — has come to my rescue. Turning my head, I see his round face and flinging my arms around his legs, I pull him down beside me.

"She's here!" he shouts triumphantly. "I'll bring her to the gap."

Bert helps me to my feet. Slowly we work our way down the side of the hedge. He leads me to the small gap they found while I was trapped. It isn't a very large gap, and Bert only got to my side with much effort and scratching on his arms and legs. We both make it back through and now the six of us are standing together, hugging each other over and over. The boys give me the remains of the supplies — a few crumbs in a screw of newspaper and the last swallow of water. They taste like a feast and now I don't feel sick.

We are crossing the first of the fields, about to climb a hedge, when the heavens open. The rain lashes and the wind blows, and I can hardly stay upright. Jack puts his arm through mine and pulls me along. We duck down and sit under a hedge to shelter but it is no good:

within seconds we are all soaked, the wee now burning my legs.

"Come *on*." Harry once again is taking command. "We can't just sit here: we'll get cold."

We fight our way across the field and over the fence. As quickly as it came the storm is gone and we walk down the school drive, this time heading for the road. It is getting dark. My plaits have come loose and wet hair clings to my face; my jumper seems to have grown several sizes; my shoes squelch on wet leaves; but above all my legs are so sore that I can hardly walk. We try to pull our clothes straight, but it is no good: the harder we try the worse we look.

"We can't tell them that we have been to the camp or we'll get into terrible trouble," whispers Harry.

"Let's just say that we got lost in the fields behind the school," Jack suggests.

"We'll get in trouble for being there, but not as much as being at the camp," Arthur mumbles through chattering teeth.

I am too tired to join in. We walk slowly up the hill towards the village and now I can see the falling ends. Up ahead are two cars, with hooded lights, and there stands Constable White with his torch shining into the darkness.

"I wonder what's happening," says Mike.

Constable White hurries towards us. "They're here, they're all here!"

I burst into loud, scared tears as a soldier gets out of an army jeep. Constable White picks me up. He tells me not to cry and passes me gently into someone's arms. It is Father.

I am so surprised that I stop crying and nestle into Father's shoulder.

"Where the heck have you been?" he asks Jack, clipping him on the ear.

Bert and George are crying now.

"If you don't stop crying, I'll give you something to cry about," snaps Constable White. "Come on. I'll walk you lot home." He wheels his bicycle round to where a group of people is huddled and we all start back to the village.

Back at home Mother takes off my soaked clothes. The rip in the jumper is not even mentioned. Father brings the big bath, filled with hot water, Mother pours in Dettol and in I go. Jack goes after me. The water makes my skin prickle but it is so good to be home that I don't complain.

The next morning I can't move my arms and legs. They are stiff and they hurt. I feel as if they're being pricked by a thousand needles. Jack is hovering around my bed; he has a great big scratch on his face. Mother tells him to leave me to rest and tells me to stay where I am.

"You've got to stay in bed. The nurse put some ointment on your scratches last night and she said that you shouldn't do anything at all today except rest."

I look down at my arms. Deep-down scratches stretch from my elbow along to my fingers and Mother tells me there is a very large one across my back. When Aunt Lily comes to see me later that morning, she tells me off for being such a tomboy. Waggling a finger at me, she tells me to stop climbing trees — otherwise I will have so many scars that I will never be a lady.

I am just about to tell her I didn't climb any trees and that I don't want to be a lady when I see Jack behind her, pulling a "don't tell" face and flapping his arms. I solemnly promise Aunt Lily that I won't climb any more trees. "Those days are over," I tell her. She seems satisfied and goes downstairs for a cup of tea. As soon as she is gone, Jack scoots to my side to fill me in. As planned, Harry told Constable White that we'd got lost. He said that I had climbed a tree to find out where we were but had missed my footing and fallen, landing in some bushes. Bert had bravely waded into the bushes and rescued me. I feel cross that Bert comes out as the hero of our adventure and not me, but as all our parents and Constable White seem to believe the story I don't let on.

Our secret safe, Harry wants to go back and explore the camp properly. He questions me about what I saw and thinks up ways of getting past the soldiers and the dogs. But before we know it, school starts again and there is no time to answer any more of Harry's questions.

Then one morning in the playground a whisper goes round that Mrs Meeks wants to see us all in the large classroom before lessons. She tells us to settle down quickly and then introduces Constable White, who is looking very serious.

"Children." The silence vibrates with his voice. "You all know that there are some German prisoners of war at the military camp on the edge of our village. These prisoners are guarded day and night by our soldiers and it is almost impossible for them to get out." He pauses and looks us over. "But last night it seems that somehow some of the prisoners managed to escape."

A cold feeling runs down my spine. Is this my fault? Did the prisoners see our gap and break out through it? Meanwhile, Mrs Meeks is telling the school — now buzzing with this dreadful news — to calm down. Constable White holds up his hand and everyone falls silent.

"If you see anyone strange in the village, do not talk to them. Tell your parents or an adult. We don't want you to be frightened, but until we catch them do not — I repeat, do not — go wandering around in the fields. We don't know if they are dangerous."

I spend the rest of the day in panic and get into a lot of trouble for not paying attention. When the day ends, I am one of the first out. It's agony waiting for Jack to come home and I hop around the houseplace, getting on Mother's nerves. The moment I hear the door, I leap on him.

"Have you heard?" I hiss. He makes his "don't speak" face.

"Mother, can Dot and I go to Arthur and Bert's? We think they need help with something," asks Jack.

"No, you may not," snaps Mother. "Go and get your school clothes off and eat this tea. Then you can play with Bob. He hasn't seen you all day. And besides," she adds, "some prisoners have escaped from the camp, so no wandering off. We don't want you getting murdered."

We go outside and play horses with Bob, his favourite game. Jack is the horse and as we tie the string to his arms, we talk about the escaped prisoners. Bob climbs on Jack's back, I take the string reins and together we make Jack gallop around the garden. Bob squeals in delight, slapping his own bottom to make Jack go faster. "Giddy yup," commands Bob.

After what seems like miles of trotting and galloping, we scurry down the road as fast as we can. The streets seem more deserted than usual. Bert and Arthur are still eating their tea. Their mother tells us to wait.

We sit on their doorstep, huddled together against the cold wind. In the gathering gloom we see Constable White's bike propped against the side of the paper shop.

"I hope it's not our fault that the Germans escaped," I whisper to Jack.

Before he can answer, the constable runs out from behind the shop. At the same moment some army jeeps come roaring up the road, a blare of horns shattering the silence. They screech to a standstill. Soldiers leap out and within seconds two giant dogs are pulling ahead of them on leashes. We jump to our feet. Bert and Arthur — cramming the remains of jam sandwiches into their mouths — fall out of the door and on to us.

"What's happening?" Bert shouts, spraying us with crumbs.

A loud voice sounds out. "Hey! You children. Get back inside *now!*"

We don't need telling twice as we tumble backwards into the twins' house. Their mother is looking out of the window and as one we head for a place beside her. Five pairs of eyes peer towards the shop.

Two soldiers appear from the back of the shop, carrying something we can't identify. Another soldier and the constable come out from inside the shop, accompanied by the man and woman who own it. The man gets into one of the jeeps with a soldier and is driven off while the woman stands talking to Constable White. Jack, Bert, Arthur and I look at each other, our mouths open in surprise. Are they German spies after all?

"They've caught him," says Arthur as we turn from the window.

"Caught who?" asks the twins' mother, mopping sweat from her face. She is a large lady and, like Bert, only moves when necessary.

But now moving for Bert is necessary. We need to know if our worst fears have been realised.

"Come *on!*" calls Arthur as he heads towards the back door.

We shoot along the back of the row of houses, down the alleyway at the side of the last house and on to the road. We are now several houses further down the road and the soldier, who still stands behind the clothes shop with a dog, does not appear to have noticed us. I stand next to Jack — the memory of those long teeth in that enormous mouth makes me shudder. Also, I don't want to go too near Constable White, who is now standing beside the soldier. If he sees us, he may remember that we were the children who had been lost in the fields near the camp and then — as adults do — he might put two and two together and think that we have something to do with the prisoners escaping.

The boys don't seem to have any such fears and are across the road, joining people who are gathering around the policeman.

"Nothing to worry about," I can hear him calling. "Please all go back to your homes now."

We hold back to see if we can find out what has happened and why our clothes shop man has been taken away. We piece snatches of overheard conversation together and soon have the story.

The prisoners stole some overalls from a washing line in the village and threw their prisoner clothes under the shop. The man from the clothes shop saw the two men in overalls walking past the shop when he arrived to open up. He noticed them as they were young and there are not many young men left in the village who are not in uniform. He was only taken away so that he can talk to an officer at the camp to make sure that the men he saw are the escaped prisoners.

Over the next few days we hear that all the German prisoners are back in the camp. One took longer to track down, as he made it across the moors. When Arthur and Bert's father comes home on leave, they tell him all about the escaped prisoners. He hopes the man from the clothes shop is in prison, calling him a "bloody conchie". We ask Father what a "bloody conchie" is, thinking it must be a war word for a wounded spy. He tells us that it means a conscientious objector.

As I get into bed that night, I ask Mother what that means, as she knows all about words, spellings and those sort of things.

"It means that his conscience tells him that he should object to going to war to kill other people. Like your Uncle Bill." As she speaks, she brushes my hair.

As she is in talking mood, I risk another question. "What is a conscience?"

She holds the brush still, my long hair heavy in her hands. "Oh, I don't know — you do ask some questions! I suppose it's what he believes in, what he's been taught, and what he has accepted as right."

I don't understand. You get put in prison if you go to war and you get put into prison if you don't go to war.

"I don't think that soldiers should go to war. Will they put me in prison?" I ask.

Pulling me to her, she gives me one of her rare hugs.

"I hope not." Her voice is low as she speaks into my hair. "I do hope not."

CHAPTER
FIVE

Changing times

April — October 1941

Grandma Compton seems to be crying a lot. Her eyes are always red and her cheeks all streaky. But I don't see her actually cry until the day Uncle Jim goes off to the war. We stand outside the house, watching as he marches past us. He is with some other men who have turned into soldiers: some who are already soldiers, including Arthur and Bert's dad, who are going back from being on leave — and others who are leaving the village for the first time, including the milkman and the man from the hardware shop. It doesn't matter if they are old soldiers or new soldiers: everyone seems to be crying. The twins' mother leans heavily on Grandma's arm, tears rolling down her ashen face. Grandma has her apron up over her face. I think she is hiding more tears. I don't like it when grown-ups cry, so I run up the road with the rest of the gang to watch Uncle Jim and the other soldiers from our village as they make their way to an army lorry at the falling ends.

A man steps out in front of me and I have to stop. For a moment I don't recognise him. He is wearing a thick uniform and he is green and sturdy instead of grey and flimsy. The April sun is shining on his polished boots. He looks back at the woman standing in the doorway of the house. She is holding a baby in her arms and three other children squeeze around her on the pavement. They are wearing trousers now, along with their jumpers, but they still have no shoes. With a grunt the man bends forward and kisses the woman's face. He places his hand across his children's heads. He doesn't seem to want to leave, but as one of the men shouts his name, he falls into line and is up off the road. He turns to look for his family but the woman is already in the house. Before the door slams, I hear her mutter, "Good riddance. I hope he doesn't come back."

When the men reach the army lorry, they climb through the back canvas. I don't think there can be enough room for them all, but still they keep tumbling on in. When all the men are on board, there is a hoot and hands appear out of the back, waving. We chase after them, shouting and cheering, as the lorry disappears.

The boys keep running. I want to go back to see how Grandma is. She is walking up the path to her front door with the twins' mother hanging on her arm. The door opens and Auntie Betty steps out, putting her arms around her mother's shoulders and guiding the two women through the doorway. She ignores me as I slide in behind them. The room is full. Grandfather is sitting in his armchair by the fire, smoke billowing from his pipe. My mother is standing beside him and as the three women enter she steps forward, her arms held out. I can hear them talking but when the grandfather clock chimes I can't make out the words. Grandfather rises and as he reaches the door, I hear him mumble, "Think men'd never been to war before."

My favourite aunt, Aunt Flo, has just stepped through the stair-foot door. She is the cause of some tears too: she is also going to join the army.

"Hello, Dolly," she says. "Has Jim gone, then? Seems to me we might need some refreshments in there."

She flourishes a large pair of scissors and cuts some leaves that are hanging in a bunch from the ceiling; then she disappears into the houseplace for the kettle. There are loads of flowers and leaves up there. I know, because I have helped Grandma to gather them. The ladies of the village say she is a "healer" and can make people better. This is good, because it costs half a crown to go the doctor, and that, Mother says, is more than the cost of the week's groceries at the Co-op. When we are feeling ill, Father visits Grandma and comes home with a strong-tasting medicine or a hot poultice. Now I can smell an aniseed sort of smell as Aunt Flo returns with a large brown jug with steam rising from it.

"I think we'll have a drop of Grandad's cough medicine in this, don't you, Dolly?"

She winks at me as she lifts down a large bottle with a picture of a man striding out across its front.

Two more ladies arrive. They live on the other side of the Sheffield Road. They are relatives of Grandma and they also watched the man of their family climb into the army lorry earlier. The crying had stopped but it starts up again, and Auntie Flo puts some more cough medicine into the jug. After a little while the medicine seems to work and everyone mostly stops crying.

A few days later, I wish I had some medicine with me at school. I am in the playground when I come across a very thin, stretched-out boy who let me hang my coat under his on the first day of term when I was lost and new. I don't know his name and I haven't spoken to him since that first day, but I have watched him in the playground, where he is always doing daring things like climbing on to the lavatory roof and hanging upside down. Inside myself I call him Long Grey Jumper, as his jumper goes right down past his knees.

He is facing the wall with his shoulders down, as if he is looking at his feet. I stop by him and creep as near as I dare. His face is red and puffy and I am sure he is crying. I try to speak to him in as bright a voice as I can manage.

"Hello."

He kicks the wall but does not speak. I try again. This time, he snarls as he turns his swollen face towards me.

"Bugger off."

I jump back. As he kicks the wall again, his shoe splits open at the toe and he leans on the wall and looks down at his foot. I stand my ground and watch. He doesn't move but I can see his shoulders going up and down. For a moment I don't know what to do, but then I remember the apple in my pocket.

"Here you are. Have this."

He grabs the apple. For a moment I think he is going to throw it at me but instead he growls:

"When I say bugger off, I mean bugger off!"

He swings round and hits the wall with his fist, kicking it again with even greater force. Then he turns and shouts to the playground:

"You can all bugger off! See if I care."

He runs towards the group of children who have come to see what is happening, thrashing his arms, punching out. As he sends them all running, shouts and squeals come from those in the firing line. One of the teachers wades through the children and tries to grab the boy, but he lashes out and drives her back. Mrs Meeks and the school caretaker appear. The headmistress puts up her hand. I hold my breath.

"You! Stop right there. I will not tolerate this silly behaviour."

But even the headmistress can't stop him.

"Bugger off, you silly old bag."

Now the caretaker steps forward.

"Hey, hey, *hey*! No need for language like that, young man."

At this, Long Grey Jumper kicks the caretaker in the shins. By now the whole school is watching. The caretaker darts forward, lands him a resounding clip around the ear and then headlocks the boy under his arm, lifting him off the floor. My last view of Long Grey Jumper is his whirling legs as he disappears into the school. He still has my apple in his hand and summoning up all the courage I have, I call out:

"You can eat the apple, Long Grey Jumper."

The playground is buzzing. The children who didn't see what happened gather around. I shrink back, thinking it might have been my fault for not buggering off in the first place. The questions fly up into the air:

"What happened?"

"Why did he kick the caretaker?"

"What will happen to him?"

From the midst of the crowd comes a voice: "His dad's dead."

For a moment there is silence and I don't know what to do with myself. Eventually, the noise starts up again. One boy remains standing on the spot. He is friends with Long Grey Jumper.

"Is his dad really dead?" I ask him.

"Du'n know. Just my mam said his mam got a telegram yesterday afternoon and that means his dad is dead."

After a day that never seems to end I get home as fast as I can, my heart beating wildly. What if my mother has received a telegram while I have been at school?

As I come round the corner to my house, I can see my father loading coal into a wheelbarrow on the side of the road. He hasn't washed yet from the pit and his face is all black, the bit around his mouth pink from where he has wiped it after drinking. I run so hard towards him that I fall over on the pebbled pavement. He raises his eyes from the silent work and looks at me. My knees are bleeding.

"What's the matter with you? Can't you ever walk? If you get blood on those socks, you'll be in for trouble."

I don't approach him but stand and watch as he fills the barrow with some of his monthly load of coal. I spit on my finger and as I wait for the moment to speak, I wipe it on my knee.

"I thought you were dead."

"Whatever made you think that?"

He looks me straight in the eye as he bends his knees to lift the handles of the loaded wheelbarrow. I walk behind him as he pushes the barrow along the alley and into our yard. He puts the handles down and stands upright.

"Long Grey Jumper's dad is dead."

Father has a large lump of coal in both his arms. I watch the muscles move under his shirt as he carries the coal into the coalhouse.

"Who says he is dead?"

"His mam got a telegram."

He looks down at me. Then, without speaking, he bends and lifts me up into his arms.

In the kitchen Mother is not too pleased.

"Look at the colour of you! Washday isn't 'til next week, Dot. You know you need to keep clean," she complains as she peels me from my father. Then, when she sees my tear-stained cheeks, she says more kindly, "Whatever is the matter?"

I tell them the story and Mother brushes me down and straightens my clothes. She puts ointment on my knees. We talk a little about people dying in the war. Later that evening Father brings the shoe last, a hammer and a square of leather out from the back of the pantry. He spends most of the evening shut in the

66

kitchen away from us. When I wake up, a pair of stoutly soled shoes is by the front door. Mother says that Father will take them down to the school after he comes home from the mine. I hope the caretaker doesn't cross Long Grey Jumper again. Father always puts a few metal studs at the heels and toes of our shoes, just to help with the wear.

It seems that we are all helping each other a bit more. Because so many of the men have gone away, the women have to do some of their jobs. Some have gone to work in factories and a woman has to carry all the heavy boxes in the Co-op. Aunt Betty is helping out at the hardware shop as well running the Post Office. A lady now drives the milk cart. She makes the horse walk very slowly and I am sure he doesn't like it. I try to stroke his nose whenever I can and I tell him the milkman will be back very soon.

The whole village seems slower and quieter, and I feel that I should whisper when I am out on the road, or even in our garden. When, one Saturday morning, Harry and Mike burst into our garden, talking together, Arthur, Bert, Jack and I are startled by the cacophony of their voices.

"We are going to have a siren in the village," says Harry, panting.

"A *what?*" we all ask at once.

"I don't know. But Dad told Mum that we are going to have a siren." Harry's father, like our father, works at the local pit and like our father is in the ARP.

Jack suggests we go and ask him.

"What do you want to know about sirens for?" Father asks.

"Harry's dad said we are having one," Jack replies.

Father looks at Mother and she raises her eyes to the ceiling, shaking her head — no.

"We'll get a letter about it when we need to know."

But Jack is not to be fobbed off with this.

"Yes, but what *is* it? I mean, what does it look like? What does it *do*?"

Father looks at Jack, who is dancing from foot to foot in front of him, and then he looks back to his paper, which lies unopened on his lap. I stand behind Jack and a line of faces look around me from the doorway. With a sigh Father takes his newspaper and mug of tea, rises from his chair and heads for the door.

"Come on, then. Let's have a talk about it."

He sits on an upturned box, which we have been playing with on our little lawn. A blue delphinium and golden iris rise behind him, and butterflies dance over his head. The boys gather around him and sit on the grass. I don't like butterflies, so I stand at the edge of the lawn.

"You know we might have bombs dropped on us?" asks Father.

He pauses and takes a sip of tea. The boys look at his face, each patiently awaiting some new revelation. We've known this for ages. Even I, in my lowly position, have been told this at school.

"Some towns have already been badly hit." He lifts his tea and takes another sip.

68

The boys now start to fidget. If we don't already know from school, we know from the endless reports on the wireless. Our wireless is on a great deal these days and sometimes Mother listens so hard that she forgets we are in the room.

"If aeroplanes are coming over to bomb us, we need to be told before they get here."

We have to wait to see what this has to do with the siren, as Father has now got out his pipe, and knocked it on his shoe. This means that he is going to fill up its bowl with tobacco; spend forever waiting for the match to burn well; draw the flame through the tobacco; check a dozen times to see if it is burning to his satisfaction; and then draw on it to send sweet-scented smoke into the air. I have waited for the end of this process on many occasions and know that it is no good trying to interrupt him. Somehow all the team knows, and the boys just sit and I lean on the wall and we wait. At last when nothing more seems to be coming, Mike risks a word.

"Why do we need to know?"

Father looks at him in surprise as if the answer is obvious.

"So that we can go somewhere safe before the bombs drop on us."

We need more. Jack wants information on the siren. He sits up on his knees and speaks into Father's face.

"But what's the *siren* got to do with it?"

Father puts his hand on Jack's head and lowers him to a sitting position.

"When the German planes are spotted, heading our way, the siren will be started and it will make so much noise that everyone in the village will hear it and all the people will be able get to somewhere safe before the bombs drop on us."

I have crept as near to the group as the butterflies will allow.

"But what is it and *where* is it?" I ask.

"I don't know what it looks like," replies Father, "but I do know that they are putting it across the road. I think they are going to put it on the top of a post by the paper shop. It will stand on the piece of land next to the clothes shop."

It is as though a bolt of electricity passes through the six of us. We each know what the other is thinking. We are still certain that the people who run the clothes shop are German spies and this surely is more confirmation. We know what we must do.

"Can we go and look at it?" Jack asks.

"I don't think there is much to see, but I suppose you can go and look if you don't get in anyone's way."

We race on to the street. At the side of the clothes shop stands a new, very tall, wooden pole. Running up it there are wires, which come from a green box next to the paper shop. It all looks rather boring.

Harry lifts a wire that is hanging from the green box and I almost jump out of my skin as a voice booms:

"Don't you go touching that box and them wires! They're dangerous — full of electricity they are."

I spin around and almost crash into a large man. He is wearing blue overalls, and tipping my head back I can

70

just about see his unshaven chin jutting out beneath the rim of a strange-looking blue cap. There is another man with him. Both are wearing leather gloves and have caps on their heads. The big man puts his hand on Harry's head and turns him around.

"Be off now. It is dangerous round here and we don't want children hanging around."

The other man lowers himself and growls into my face. He smells of cigarettes.

"Grr, grr, be off."

We can still hear them laughing as we fall behind Bert and Arthur's front garden wall.

"That was a close shave!" says Harry.

We peer around the wall. One of the men has now climbed up the post and the other is holding wires in his hands. We move to the steps of the house and, sitting in two rows, we study their every movement. They are now taking the wires up the post and fastening them to its top.

"They've got very funny uniforms on. Our dad doesn't wear one like that," says Arthur.

"*Germans!*" hisses Harry.

Now we have proof that the clothes shop owners have German soldiers working for them.

Bert says, "I've read in a comic that they use a wireless to send messages to each other."

Jack is a Cub Scout and knows lots about secret messages. "They have wires like those to tap Morse code messages to each other," he explains gravely.

As soon as the men have finished their work and ridden off on bicycles, we set off across the road. The green box is completely sealed and the wires are firmly attached to the pole. It looks even more boring than before and after we have walked past the box a few times, given it a sly kick and even pushed it, we are at a loss as to what to do next. We decide we will all watch it when we can and report back if we see anything suspicious.

We watch it at different times of the day, Jack and I even sneaking out late one evening to see if anything is going on. But the pole just stands there and the wires remain in the green box.

It is on a Saturday afternoon that the siren first sounds. Saturday afternoon tea is important to Mother. The best china always comes out of the cupboard and is placed on a clean white tablecloth. Now Jack and I are helping her lay the table and Mother brings over a plate of thinly sliced, buttered bread and a glass dish containing plum jam. The smell of apple rings and stewing prunes has been filling the house all morning and these Mother places in an ornate glass bowl. Today we also have a wobbly red jelly — the mould has been standing in a bowl of cold water in the sink — and caraway seed cake.

Mother looks up at the face of the railway clock. We always have tea at four-thirty on Saturday.

"Hmm, I don't think he is going to make it."

The last of the summer sun shines through the window and makes the china and glass sparkle. At this moment, our small houseplace with its dark furniture and brown linoleum floor looks like a palace.

Mother sighs as she pulls out the chair at the end of the table.

"Wash your hands and come and sit down."

She almost whispers the words but they hold power, more power than if she had shouted. Aunt Lily came over earlier to tell Mother that she had heard that Father was doing a "double back shift" and I suppose this is why Father isn't here. The four of us sit to eat in silence, Father's place at the head of the table noisy in its emptiness.

Just as we are tucking into the prunes, I think I hear a low wailing noise coming from outside. Before I can say anything, the noise gets louder and louder, until it feels as if the walls of the house are shaking. It is so loud that I can't even hear Bob crying. Jack and I look at Mother. She is speaking but we can't hear her either. We lip-read.

"It's the siren," she mouths. "Stay there."

She picks Bob up and runs through the kitchen to the outside door. But we can't sit still and are off our chairs, following her out on to the road. There are lots of people looking up at the post. The noise seems to be coming from a small grey box at the top. I can see them talking, but no one can hear anything anyone else is saying and some people have put their hands over their ears as if to defend themselves from the attack. It is clear that no one knows what to do.

Suddenly the noise drops and people are left shouting into their neighbour's face. But no sooner has the wailing died down than it starts up again. It wails out two more times before it finally stops. Father stands with his arm around Mother's shoulders. In all the commotion we hadn't seen him arrive.

As an ARP warden, he knows what is happening. He tells everyone: "Three blasts on the siren is the warning that planes are coming. When it's all over, we get one long blast and that's the all clear. It has to be this loud so that the entire village can hear it. It will have to wake us up at night when everyone is sound asleep. This is just a test to see how we all react. They are also going to try it out at night, when we will all be obliged to get up and go to our shelters."

We file back to our homes. Father has a quick wash and we eat, the noise of the siren still ringing in my ears. Jack is full of questions.

"Where will we go? Do we have a shelter?"

Mother screws up her face. "No. We are going under the stairs. We have put some mattresses under the stone benches and we can sleep on those."

"George and Harry have got a large hole in their garden. Their dad and their uncle dug it. They say that that's a shelter," Jack informs us.

Mother interrupts her tea-pouring to give Jack a fierce stare. "I don't care what anyone says: I'm not crawling into any cold, damp hole. If I have to die, I'll do it in a dry place. Now be quiet and eat your tea."

We forget about the siren until we hear it in the night. I am startled awake and sit up. It is dark and there is a tremendous noise shaking my bed.

Father stands over me, pulling me to standing as he drags a blanket up behind me and grabs me; then he turns and runs. I am whirling head first down the stairs as he calls into my ear:

"Keep your head tucked in, Dolly."

Taking the three stone steps in one stride, Father takes me into the pantry. Two candles are burning in the alcove under the stairs. I can see Mother's back: she is bending over and pushing something under the stone bench. Father sits me down on the bench behind her. Her lips are moving but I can't hear anything.

Suddenly we are both spinning around again and I am facing the dark end of the alcove. My feet knock against metal, Father releases his hold and I fall feet first. I try to grab his shirt, but the blanket has fastened my arms. My fall is checked and for a moment I watch Mother over a dark wall as she kneels on the stone floor. The candle on the bench beside her throws a pale, elongated shadow of her head on the wall above me, and as the fall begins again and I sink below the dark wall, the shadow flickers and dances above me. Everything goes dark.

I wake up. I try to stand, but I can't: there is nothing to press my feet against. So I shout as loudly as I can:

"Mother! Father! I'm here."

Hands lift me and I stand on the cold pantry floor. It is morning. I have slept. My place in our strange shelter was the dolly tub, in which Mother washes and which over the week fills up with soiled clothes.

The dolly tub becomes my place of safety whenever we hear the siren and I get used to it pretty quickly, even when I have to bed down among a pile of unwashed clothes.

CHAPTER
SIX

They pass. They don't stay with us

May 1942

Jack and I need to get out of the house.

Mother is in the middle of a washday, a ferocious six hours of toiling and boiling, of steam and heat, of soap and soda that makes breathing difficult. Father lit the copper in the corner of the kitchen before he went to work and it has been bubbling madly all morning. We are sitting on the settee while Mother — her sleeves rolled up, her hair pasted to her head — goes backwards and forwards, taking the hot water from the boiler by the fire in the houseplace into the kitchen, her face getting redder and redder with each bucket. We hear her cries of "Damn it! Damn it!" while she wields the wooden punch, pushing the sheets, clothes and towels into the dolly tub, the water foaming and splashing. As she throws herself on to a dining chair and lifts her apron to wipe her sweating face, we strike.

"Can we call for Bert and Arthur?"

"Go," says Mother, panting. "But stay around the green: don't go wandering away. There's a large convoy coming through today, and they won't want you in the way."

We'd rather be in the way out there than in the way in here. We don't want to be here when she lifts the sheets from the boiling water to be rinsed in the sink. Nor when she rolls the dolly under the big mangle, whose large wooden rollers, I am frequently told, could crush the life out of me. Nor when the smell of bleach makes our eyes water as the towels soak in the baby bath. No, we want to come back when the hard work is done and the sheets are pegged on the clothes line running down the garden, when the crack of the clean laundry in the wind makes Mother smile for the first time all day.

We make a run for it.

"*What's* coming?" I ask Jack.

There are people on the road and I am startled when I almost collide with a group of soldiers. They aren't from our village and for a moment I stand motionless, trying to make sense of things. I grasp Jack's sleeve.

"What are they?"

Jack doesn't sound too sure. "I think they are our soldiers."

"Are they going to start fighting the Germans in the camp?

Jack is not his usual assured self and his reply is hesitant: "I don't know."

The road itself looks different. It is full of strangers. I look up and down at the people, thinking I must be in a dream. I turn to ask Jack to pinch me but he is gone. Then I see Father. At least I think it is Father. He isn't wearing his pit clothes and as I get closer, I see that he is wearing his ARP uniform. Even he looks different.

I've only seen him wear the helmet and armband before now. He is standing with some soldiers, talking to Jack.

"Mind you stay on this side of the road, both of you; there's a very long convoy coming in about an hour. If you get caught on the other side of the road, you won't be able to get back until they've gone through. It could take several hours to pass and I don't want you two caught on the other side of the road."

Father's voice is very stern. Whatever is it that is coming? It sounds very dangerous to me, and I'm not sure if I want to be on any side of the road when it comes.

"Are you coming with us?" I ask Father.

"No. I have to stay and help the soldiers direct it through the village."

"Where will it go?"

One of the soldiers says, "It will go to the camp at the other side of the village."

I peer up at his face. He looks as though he knows a thing or two, so I ask on.

"Will it stay there for a long time? Will it live there?"

"I told you," says Father: "you only have to cough, and Miss Chatterbox here has got six questions to ask on why you did it."

The soldier laughs and I feel very silly. I should have taken my chance and asked the one question that matters.

"Off you go now, and behave yourselves," says Father.

He pushes my back and I run after Jack, who is already heading down the road. Bert and Arthur are standing on the pavement outside their house. They look as though they are in some sort of trance.

"What's happening?" asks Bert.

We give them all the information we have.

"What *is* a convoy?" I ask again.

"I suppose Harry would know," says Arthur.

On down the road the four of us race, to see if Harry is available to have his brain picked. We don't have far to go before we spot him and his brother, George, standing at the falling ends. They are watching the soldiers as they erect barriers across the roads. Harry greets us with a broad smile.

"Good, isn't it?"

"But what's coming?" I ask.

George replies with great authority. "A convoy."

This is taking me around in circles; I still have not had an answer. So in a defeated tone I ask again: "But what *is* a convoy?"

At last an answer comes. Harry puffs himself up.

"It's a lot of men walking in a long line behind each other. Like those pictures on the newsreels when they show soldiers walking behind each other. They are a convoy. Some ride on lorries." He finishes his explanation with a flourish, like a teacher finishing a lesson.

Well, now I know, and it doesn't sound too scary. I wonder what it is that Father is getting so excited about.

A policeman puts his arm across and pushes us backwards.

"Move back. Move out of the way, please. They are going to put a barrier across here."

All the roads, except the one we came down and the one leading east out of the village, are now barricaded. We can't stand still, as we are too excited, so we all go back up the road to fetch Mike.

Jack tells him, "We can't go to the other side of the road."

"Why not?" asks Mike.

We repeat what Father said, but George is suddenly excited and argumentative.

"Bet I could get across."

"You won't when the convoy comes. Mother had to go across to the shop half an hour ago to do her shopping. Constable White was up the road telling everyone they wouldn't be able to cross the road until late this afternoon," says Bert.

As he speaks there is a blaring of car horns and two jeeps speed past us. We look up and down the road expectantly, but nothing comes. George is not going to be thwarted by such an incident.

"I bet the soldiers will walk in a line on the pavement, so it won't matter if we cross the road."

Before we can say another word he has darted into the road and the next time we see him he is standing on the pavement at the other side, laughing at us. Back across he shoots and stands by us.

Harry shouts at him. "You mustn't do that, George!"

We all try to hold him, but with an almighty tug he pulls himself free and goes back across the road. We see him stumbling forward as he loses his step on the far pavement, but before we have time to see what has happened to him, a green lorry bears down on us with its horn blaring. A soldier in the jeep is calling through a loud hailer.

"Keep the road clear! Keep the road clear!"

People have gathered on both sides of the street. It is strange to see so many people in our village all standing together. I didn't know this many people were still here. We look across the road. George is nowhere to be seen. Harry shouts his name but is soon silenced by a rumbling noise that is rising from afar. It grows in volume and fills the air, until the sound seems to be inside us and the pavements begin to shake.

A monstrous vehicle crawls over the brow of the hill, filling both sides of the road. Clutching Jack's hand, I retreat. The women, who have been standing gossiping at the side of the road, scurry back and peer round their shawls at what is coming. At its front the vehicle is like a lorry, but at its back metal tracks grind around its wheels. I have seen pictures of tanks and now here they are in our village, like something from space comics, where green men from Mars drive them across a moonscape. I watch in awe as several crawl past us. I become braver when the jeeps pass, and moving forward again I stand by the roadside. At last the jeeps finish passing and the road is quiet. In the excitement we have forgotten George, but Harry hasn't and knows that he must find his brother.

"Where's George? Where's George?"

He is shouting as we run up and down on the pavement, trying to look at the other side, but the women, who are now feeling braver, are standing on the pavement edge and we can't see past them.

"I could go across and look for him," Harry shouts.

But we hold on to him, for now a new noise is filling the air. It sounds like a huge caterpillar munching its way towards us, and once again we retreat. It seems that everyone from the village is standing by the roadside, waiting to see what will come over the hill. A cheer sounds further up the road and some boys start to run towards us.

Then over the hill they come, rows and rows of men. Two soldiers in light uniforms stride in front and then in lines of eight they march towards us. For a moment we are silent, and then a shout goes up and everyone begins to clap and to cheer. A great noise and excitement fill the air, like the ringing of bells. Then as they near us, the soldiers seem to overwhelm everything. The road is full from side to side; there is a sea of faces over a mass of khaki, and the stones on the road sing.

I have no idea how many men march past us, but they take most of the day to pass. Sometimes individual faces become clear, a tired look or a smile; sometimes we see a wave, or, from the edge of the column, a hug, or a kiss. Mother and several other women make large jugs of tea, which some soldiers stop to take. Others pass over their tin mugs and drink as they march, though I think they spill most of it. Father drinks with some of them when they stop to check how far they must march, and we children get patted on the head a lot.

"These are our boys. They are going to fight the Germans," says Jack, proudly.

I look at the mass of men passing by. They don't look like boys to me. Most of them are about the same age as my father, though some do look younger, like Uncle Jim. They seem to fill the village, as if they are taking up all the room we have. We run up and down at the side of the marching men. When the front of the column reaches the falling ends by the church, it turns left and disappears down the hill, as if to leave the village.

"Where are they going?" we ask anyone who will listen to us.

"To the camp," a man at the crossroads tells us, and as that is all we can get out of him, we go back up the road and sit in silence on Bert and Arthur's steps. Mike is the first to voice the question.

"How can they go to the camp if the Germans are still there?"

We all look across at the clothes shop and wait for the convoy to finish passing. The noise of the boots on the road is loud and I begin to think that all the men in England must be marching through our little village.

It seems like hours later when a policeman leads a tear-stained George across the road. Harry gets his ear filled for not taking proper charge of his younger brother. We also come in for some of the stick, but we are so pleased to see George back unscathed that we take it on the chin and even hug him when the policeman has gone.

"Well, what camp do you think they are going to?" Arthur mumbles.

"Let's go and ask Father," says Jack.

Mike thrusts his face into Jack's and, with a low sneer in his voice, pushes him backwards.

"We can't, you idiot. He might start asking how we know about the Germans."

But we set off and when we catch up with Father, he smiles down on me and I put my hand in his.

"Which camp will the soldiers go to?" I ask in my sweetest voice.

I see the boys pulling faces behind Father.

"As far as I know they are being billeted in the camp just out of the village." He nods his head in the direction of the camp where we are sure the German prisoners live.

"Will they go and fight the Germans?" I ask.

Now the boys are almost exploding, but Father seems not to notice anything untoward.

"I don't know, and anyway you shouldn't be asking. That's not for us to know."

Then, as his eyes follow the last of the men who disappear down the road, he murmurs more to himself than to us, "But I expect they are going somewhere to die."

I don't ask any more: Father looks too sad, and the boys are keen to get me away before I start letting the cat out of the bag. Plus we don't want to attract too much attention to ourselves, as it is getting rather late and we don't want to be sent home to get ready for bed. There is still a lot of activity and we don't want to miss a thing.

"We'll find out about the camp later," says Harry.

We troop back to Bert and Arthur's doorstep and watch the last of the jeeps and the last of the soldiers pass. Then our eyes rest on the clothes shop.

"I wonder if the clothes shop has been watching the soldiers," whispers George. "I bet they have sent a message to Germany already."

Harry almost pushes his brother off the step. "Well, you were on their side of the road: you could have watched them."

George lets out a moan as he drops forward. "I couldn't see anything; I had to stand at the side of the policeman all day. He only let me go for one drink and a tiddle at somebody's house."

We all roar with laughter.

"I bet they've gone home with all these soldiers around," I say.

Mike gets some toffee from his pockets and as we sit sucking and chewing, we watch the shop. I sink into Arthur's shoulder. I am so tired that I don't feel the cold; nor do I see how dark it is. As I close my eyes, I can only hear murmurs and doors shutting as people go back inside their homes to make tea. And as the village settles back into itself, silence falls.

CHAPTER
SEVEN

The silent war of waiting, waiting in hunger

October 1942 — January 1943

The postman knocks at the back door and Jack takes a letter. We don't get post very often and Mother is down the stairs very quickly. As Jack gives her the long buff-coloured envelope she looks at its front; then, turning it over, she looks at its back. She has a strange expression on her face.

"What is it?" I ask.

She doesn't speak, continuing to stare at the envelope as she walks slowly back into the houseplace. Jack, Bob and I stand behind her as she places the envelope on the mantelpiece. After directing a long firm gaze at it, she turns as she speaks:

"I'm going to get dressed. Don't you dare touch that."

The envelope stands in its place over the fire, and when the stairs stop creaking, I ask:

"What's in it?"

Jack is pulling a chair towards the fireplace. I hold on to Bob so that he doesn't try to do the same as him.

"I don't know, but I'm going to find out."

"Jack! Jack!" I hiss, urgently. "Don't! Mother will kill you."

But Jack isn't listening. He has pulled the chair to the side of the fireguard and is now standing on it.

"It's got Father's name on it. It's got a red crown stamped on the top and some wavy red lines."

He stands on tiptoe, dangerously close to tipping over into the fire, and as I hear the stairs creak, I put Bob down and throw my arms around Jack's legs. Over he comes, chair and all. In a mass of legs — human and wooden — we twist together on the floor.

"I told you to leave that letter alone."

Tears fill Mother's eyes as she grabs Jack's arm and then mine. Pulling us away from the chair, she sends us both stumbling towards the door.

"Get out! Get out, both of you, out of my sight."

I can hear Bob crying as Mother commands him to be silent. We watch the door from the alleyway, and Bert and Arthur join us. Bert does his best to reassure us.

"Our dad got one of those, and then he had to go in the army."

With this fearful thought we await Father's return from work, and as he opens the door and wheels in his bike, we slide in behind him.

"What are you two up to?" he asks suspiciously.

Mother is standing between the kitchen and the houseplace. The curtain is drawn back and she attempts to assume a calm manner as she holds the letter out towards him.

"This came for you, Joe."

He looks at it for a long moment, and then busies himself removing his bicycle clips and coat. When the coat is hanging on its nail and his boots are standing below it, he looks at her. Her face, pale and puffy, has not moved, and she is still holding the envelope. Leaning towards her, Father kisses her forehead and puts his hand on her shoulder.

"Have you got a cup of tea there then, Nellie?"

"But the letter, Joe: aren't you going to open it?"

Father walks past her and through the doorway.

"If it's bad news it'll wash down better with a nice cup of tea. If it's good news I'll need to celebrate."

He smiles at us and, turning to the fire, checks that there is tea in the pot, lifts the kettle and pours the water, steam rising and hiding his face as he does so.

"You read it, Nellie. I won't be able to see it properly. My eyes haven't got used to the daylight yet." He doesn't look at her.

Mother opens her mouth to protest, but changes her mind. Jack, Bob and I stand like statues, hardly daring to breathe. With her long, careful fingers, Mother unseals the flap at the back of the envelope. As she stands and reads, her pale face close to the page, her lips move in silent speech. Then the silence breaks. With a roar of laughter she waves the letter in the air and throws herself at Father.

"Steady, Nellie! You'll get scalded."

He catches her in one arm. Now she has her arms round his neck and is kissing his face, coal dust and all. I am very surprised, as Mother rarely shows such emotion. Laughing, Father picks her up off her feet and swings her around.

"I'd better hope that I get some more letters. What am I celebrating?"

Mother is now pouring tea, her face flushed and smiling.

"What does the letter say, Nellie? I assume it didn't say report to the Western Front."

Mother turns and presents Father with a mug of tea.

"It's from the Ministry of Employment, or something. They want you to be on some committee, about mine safety and facilities."

Father reaches for the letter, and with the mug in one hand and the letter in the other, he settles into his armchair. The corner of the room soon fills with pipe smoke.

"Do you want a cup of tea, Dorothy?" asks Mother.

"Will Father have to go away?" I have decided the only way to get any information is to answer a question with a question.

"No, he won't have to go far. Just his old Union work."

Mother is smiling again. The morning had felt all cold and dark and small, but now the sun is shining through the window and the world is warm and big again.

Snow is falling. I watch it through the window, large flakes floating down and covering the garden before nightfall.

"Are you two going to help with these garlands?" asks Father. "We'll never get enough made if we don't get started."

Yesterday evening we cut newspaper into strips. Now the shoebox in which we had put them stands in the middle of the wooden table. The table looks bare, as if it isn't wearing anything. The next bit of our decorating will be messy, so Father has taken off the tablecloth and it hangs forlornly over the back of a chair. He busies himself in the long cupboard beside the fireplace and brings out pots of poster paint and brushes.

Bob pulls himself on to one of the chairs and his arms appear on the table.

"What colour shall I do?" he asks.

"You paint some of the strips red and Dolly, you can paint some green. But put some newspaper down first. We don't want to get paint on the table. Your mother has enough to do; we don't want to make more work for her."

Father glances up at the ceiling. Mother has been coughing for most of the morning. When he returned home from the pit, Father coaxed a fire to burn in the bedroom and Mother — who never stops working during the day — went back to bed. Since then her coughing seems to have quietened a little.

We start painting. Bob is firm in his concentration, the tip of his little tongue poking out as he brushes the strips of newspaper. When Jack arrives home he gets on with the yellow strips. We work hard and before the daylight fades and the gaslight is lit, we have the whole box of paper strips painted and are ready to make the chain garlands. Father is standing on a chair with the hammer in his hand. Now he taps the head of the nail.

"Pass it up. Hold it up high and don't pull on it or it will rip."

The first link of the chain hangs over the nail and soon our paper chains criss-cross the room from corner to corner. Mother makes no comment on them when she comes downstairs to take some aspirin. Her face is white and her eyes are black, and she is unsteady as she walks.

Next day, we trudge to school in our warmest clothes, the snow thick on the ground. When a pipe from the boys' toilet burst, a great sheet of ice covered half the playground, and the boys have made some great slides — some starting from right at the top of the playground by the toilets, zigzagging all the way down to the door by Mrs Meeks's office. I have quickly become an expert at sliding, manipulating myself down any one of the slides top to the bottom, even though it has meant wet knickers for the rest of the day.

On the third morning of snow I arrive at school as early as I can, the slides irresistible. But now the playground is just a yellow mush. In disbelief, I ask a boy, who is kicking at some of the mush:

"What's happened?"

"I don't know. Somebody put sand, or something, on the slides."

When school starts a teacher is standing by the door to the cloakroom.

"Go into the big classroom. Mrs Meeks wants to talk to you all."

Mrs Meeks is wearing a large white bandage on her leg; the caretaker is helping her to walk and he has a very fierce look about him.

"There will be no more sliding in the school playground," she warns. "Any child caught making a slide will be severely punished."

Her head disappears and then reappears again.

"Hum, and may I wish you all a pleasant Christmas."

She stands there expectantly. One of the teachers waves her arm in the air and a rather raggedy chorus chants:

"We wish you a merry Christmas, Mrs Meeks."

We haven't practised, so there are a few variations on the "merry" part, but we all wish her something.

In the early evening, Bert, Arthur, Mike, Harry, Jack and I are carol singing, knocking on doors and trying our luck with a couple of verses of any carols we can remember from school, when a boy runs down the road towards us. White puffs of breath are coming from his mouth.

"Jack, Dot! Your dad says that you've got to go home. Something's happened to your mam."

For a moment I stand stock-still, the words of the carol still in my mouth.

Then as Jack starts running and the words become real, I am running too. My feet slip on the icy pavement and I fall to my knees, the jolt taking my breath away. But there is no time to think about myself and I am up.

The back door stands open, light floods on to the yard and people are standing around gawping. The stair-foot door is open, and for a moment I see the wooden steps that lead up to my bedroom. Then I see Father walking backwards down the stairs. Two men in brown coats are following him, and between them they are carrying Mother. She is sitting on a large canvas chair.

Father speaks, but it is not his voice. It is tight and hesitant, full of fear and uncertainty.

"Thank goodness they found you. Your mother is very ill. We have to take her to hospital."

People are moving around, their shapes black against the light from the house. Everything seems to float in front of me as if it is not real, or as if I am seeing it through someone else's eyes. I catch a glimpse of Mother's face. It is white, her eyes are closed and her lips are blue. There are so many people between us that I can't give her a kiss or even touch her hand.

Father goes with Mother in the ambulance. Jack and I stand in the yard. The door stays open. I think: where is Bob?

"Better get in before the warden comes round."

Aunt Lily stands behind us, a shawl around her shoulders. Bob is standing next to her. He throws himself into my arms. People standing in the alleyway are still peering into our house.

"Get home with you! The show's over! Nosy lot of beggars." Auntie Lily dismisses the onlookers with a wave of her hand. She considers herself a cut above the rest, and her sharp tongue leaves lesser mortals in no doubt as to her opinion of them.

The house is cold; the chill wind has got into every corner. Aunt Lily walks around the houseplace, touching ornaments and furniture, her very actions showing her disdain.

"Your father put some money in the gas meter before he went, so you should be all right."

She reaches up and pulls the chain hanging by the lampshade. The light fades and only the table shows in the dull, yellow light. She pokes the bottom of the fire, throws coal on to it and, with hands on hips, turns to face us. Her voice rings with malicious triumph.

"Well, your father has got himself in a right mess now, hasn't he? Teach him to have a possum of kids with her. I suppose she'll die and then he'll be in real trouble, won't he?"

An icy fear hits me. Mother and Father have gone. Mother will die and Father will be in trouble. We will be alone. Jack takes my hand. His chin is held high and his voice wobbles.

"We'll be all right."

"Well, you'd better be. I'm taking Bob and I can't manage any more of you. I told your father that before he went."

With this she picks up Bob and is off.

I don't know what mess Father is in, but I do know that Mother would not want Aunt Lily in our house. Of all my aunts she disapproves most of Mother not going to Chapel. Jack climbs on the table and pulls down the chain at the side of the lamp so that the gas mantel glows and the room is light.

Father comes home late. He looks very tired. The news is bad. Mother has pneumonia; she is very ill and has to stay in the hospital. Things feel a little better when we sit close on the settee and eat the fish and chips he has brought home. Father keeps rubbing his hand across his face.

"I have to go to work tomorrow and it's Christmas Eve."

For a moment, he seems to be lost in his own world. I look up at his face. I want to help. I want to take some of the fear and responsibility on to my own shoulders. But I don't know how to do it, or if I will be able to carry it if I take it.

"You'll have to go Rompton, and do what shopping you can, Dolly."

He smiles and pulls me to him. For some moments his face rests on my head and then I know what I must do. Going shopping will be my responsibility.

"Take the ration books with you, but be careful not to lose them, or we will all starve."

As Father will be gone to the pit before we wake up, he gives me Mother's purse. It has a good deal of money in it. We stow the money and the ration books in the large leather shopping bag.

"Get what you can, Dolly," he says.

The next morning, I set off to market. As large snowflakes float across my face, tears fill my eyes and I wipe them away with my sleeve. My pixie-hood is loose around my head, and a cold wind, which whirls the snowflakes into a dancing frenzy, blows around my ears. A shudder runs through me and once again I wipe my face with my sleeve. I stand at the pavement edge by the bus stop. A man and a woman are standing beside me.

"Why don't you stand nearer the wall, duck? You'll be a bit warmer there," suggests the man.

He puts his hand out as if to help me and offers me a warm smile.

The bus appears around the corner; a cloud of exhaust smoke fills the air. As I climb on to the crowded bus, standing room only, I am pushed into a woman who feels like Mother but whose face is angry. Tears fill my eyes again.

When we reach Rompton, the bus stops with a jolt. I lose my balance and am thrown into the back of a man. The woman pushes me forward.

"Come on, duck. Get off if you are going to."

I stumble down the bus steps behind the man, the large shopping bag dragging behind me. The cross woman stands on it and we both almost fall. In a tumble I cross the pavement and land by a shop wall.

"Where's your mam?" shouts the lady. "Some people can't look after their children."

Shopping for our Christmas dinner sounded possible last night, but now people push around me and the shops tower high. But I can't let Father down. He is depending on me.

Mother always begins her shopping at the market. So does everyone else, it seems. A queue wends around the stalls. In silence, women stand shoulder to shoulder in ranks firm and impenetrable. Their hats sit securely on heads, their scarves are tied tightly under chins and they look fierce as they protect their place in the queue. Dragging the bag behind me and squeezing past the women, I find the end of the queue. I have left the shelter of the stalls, and now the falling snow turns to ice-cold water as it lands at my feet. I lean sideways and look along the line, hoping it is heading towards the mounds of potatoes and parsnips that I need.

A large lady with a scarf tied over her head arrives. She stands behind me — well, not really behind me, more to the side of me — and she is very close, so close that I am squeezed out of the queue and I can't see how I am going to slide back to my place. By lowering my head and going in under her bosom, I push myself up between her and the back of the woman who is standing before me. Puffing, as if she is out of breath, the large lady talks to herself. Several times I look up to see if it's me she's talking to, but she takes no heed of me. She looks over my head, or into her purse, and is engaged in a constant little shuffle forward.

Just when I have become used to her voice and am able to ignore her closeness, she pokes me in the back of my head. I turn and, leaning back, look up. Her metal curlers glint as she glares down at me over her big bosom. Her crooked lips are pouting and her eyes are narrow and look at me as if I am, at that moment, breaking a lot of rules all at once.

"You can't stand here and save a place for your mam, you know. She's got to come and queue herself. There's no shoving in."

I try to reply but at first nothing comes. Eventually I manage a few words but they seem faint and lost against the mass of her body.

"She can't come. She's in hospital. They took her there last night."

Stepping back a little, she looks down at me. I think she is going to push me to one side, and I shrink my head down in order to avoid the blow. Several other pairs of eyes now look at me, and a low rumble runs up the queue.

The woman rubs her hand across her nose and snuffles.

"She dying?"

I nod.

A large arm comes around me and the smell of perspiration, soap and cooking — the things of life, of home, of Mother — swamp me in awful misery.

She speaks softly into the top of my head. "You stay with me. I'll see you get all you are due to, for your mam." In a louder voice, she addresses the queue. "What's the matter with you lot? You never seen a kid cry 'cause her mam's dying?"

The murmurs fade.

The queue moves forward at a caterpillar pace and after some minutes the woman asks:

"How many books you got?"

I rummage around the bottom of the bag. She takes the books from me and studies them, turning each one over in her hands.

"You should get fruit on this green one, and don't you let the man tell you anything else. You might get some on the blue ones." Waving the yellow one, she asks, "Is your dad a miner?"

I nod.

"Then you tell him, 'cause you might get a few extra potatoes. You have a right to them."

I take the books from her and look at them with awe. I had no idea that they held such information.

"Once he takes your books, it means that you are registered with him, so you can come here to shop every Saturday. He's not bad — gets as much as he can for us. He marks your books for potatoes, for carrots and certainly for onions, if he's got any. You got some coupons in there need spending. Always got coupons for sale, he has; he don't say where he got 'em. When he's had your books, you get 'em back: don't let him take 'em out of your sight. He takes all sorts out of 'em, if he gets a chance."

She smiles, revealing a mouth of brown teeth. I look at the books again. I had no idea that shopping was so complicated.

The lesson continues as we wend our way around the stalls. I become trained in the skills of ration book manipulation and well versed in the art of "turning it on."

With my friend's hand pressed firmly in my back and my heart beating loudly, I step forward. The stallholder stands before me, his hands plunged into a pocket at the front of his brown apron. He is an older, grey-haired man. His nose is red and the wiry hair on his hatless head stands high and stiff. I stand with my ration books thrust out towards him.

"We don't serve children," he snarls, putting his hand out to brush me aside.

The voice behind me booms. "Take her books, Ron, you mean bugger. Her mam is in hospital, dying. And don't you short-change her, 'cause I'm watching you, you miserly old sod."

Ron snorts. But he takes my books and the food appears without my asking. Smells of aniseed and peppermint from the next-door stall fill the air and I watch as the contents of large glass bottles are disgorged on to the shining brass scales. The coupons even run to a bar of chocolate for Mother.

I stagger from the stall with the large bag full. I have potatoes, cabbage, carrots, an onion and even apples for Christmas. The woman comes with me to the bus stop. I struggle on to the bus with my large leather shopping bag and two extra paper carrier bags.

"I'm sure your mam will be all right. With a good girl like you, I know she'll soon get better."

I try to thank her, but people are pushing me down the aisle and when I look through the back window she is nowhere to be seen.

I get the food home and Father and Jack tell me I have done very well. But Christmas is quiet and sad this year. Father spends most of the time at the hospital with Mother, as she is still very ill. At least we don't starve.

I go back to the market on the next Saturday morning. I look everywhere for my friend but she isn't in the queue for vegetables or at any of the other stalls. I have no problem with Ron. Even when a few women complain, he just ignores them.

Way after the New Year and way after we are back at school, Mother comes home from hospital. She is thin and fragile. The doctors have told her that she mustn't go outside for some weeks.

She doesn't need to. I do the shopping. I have all the skills — taught to me by my very own Christmas saviour and honed to perfection at Rompton market.

CHAPTER
EIGHT

The Yanks are coming

March — July 1943

It is unusual to hear Father talking early in the morning. Is Mother ill again? I am out of bed, down the stairs in a flash, throwing open the stair-foot door.

"What's happened? Are you all right, Mother?"

Mother's voice comes from the houseplace. "Yes, of course I am."

Jack is close on my heels.

"What's happened?"

I stand, barefooted on the stone floor, and watch Father vent anger on his tangled bootlaces. He spits out his words with the scorn that is usually reserved for strike-breakers.

"The Yanks are here."

"What are Yanks?"

Mother looks up at me, her face red after the effort of making the fire burn.

"Never you mind what Yanks are, young lady. You get ready for school."

Father swings the kettle on to the fire. Water shoots from the spout, putting the flames out. He glowers at the dark fire, his very look enough to make the flames return. Mother turns on him.

"Joe, stop getting so angry! We can't win this war on our own and you know it."

"Maybe, but what's it going cost us, Nellie?"

Father rattles the poker in the fire.

Mother holds her hands out to him, palms upwards.

"So what should we do, Joe? Lose?"

"I don't know, Nellie, but they could have come earlier, before we got so badly smashed. If we do win, and that's a big if, it will take more than our lifetime to sort things out, and it will cost us."

"I didn't start this war, Joe; nor did the Americans. We don't have to like them. All I know is, if we don't beat the Nazis you and I could be in a lot of trouble and you may never see your children grow up."

Mother's fists are clenched and her mouth is hard. For a moment Father stands and looks at her; then he swings back to the fire and attacks it with the poker.

"But they'll take the lot, you mark my words."

We go to school earlier than usual. The ash tree waves its bare branches against the sky; the road looks the same and the wind blows as cold as the day before. I was expecting something to have happened; certainly I was expecting someone to be in the village, someone whom Father doesn't welcome but whom Mother does. Who are these Yanks? They have divided my parents and I am worried, as I've never seen my parents quarrel before. I am also worried because Father said that they would take everything. I look

103

down at my worn shoes. We don't have much. Why would anyone want to take all our things?

A horn beeps loudly, and I jump to the side of the pavement.

"Hi!" a voice calls over the roar of an engine.

Waving hands emerge from the jeep and faces beam out from under khaki, metal, helmets.

"Who were *they*?" I ask.

"I don't know," says Jack.

Several jeeps pass as we walk down to the falling ends. We stop to watch each one as it goes by, and from every one comes the same greeting.

We wave and call back: "Hi!"

A few villagers wave as the soldiers call out their greeting, but for most people it is a work day and there is little time to loiter. Bert and Arthur join us and go off to school with Jack. I linger a little longer, leaning on the back of the wooden seat. Old Stan, his cap pulled down over his ears, his muffler wrapped twice around his neck, looks straight ahead.

"Who are they?" I ask. "Are they Germans?"

He doesn't reply immediately. His blue-scarred hands catch a dewdrop from his nose.

"Don't think so, lass. Somebody said as how they were Yanks. I don't know: so many buggers coming and going these days, you hardly know who you are yourself."

A few more jeeps pass. They turn down the hill and disappear eastward, towards the camp.

When I get into the school playground the news is going around that Mrs Meeks wants to see us before

104

class. With due enthusiasm, we pile into the large classroom to await her neat, grey hair. When she arrives, she is smiling broadly.

"Good morning, children," she says, beaming.

We are so amazed we can hardly manage a "Good morning" in return.

"Come on, come on! Such a good morning, you can manage better than that." She sings out again: "Good morning, children."

We all shout back as loudly as we can. "Good morning, Mrs Meeks."

"Now, children, we have some very special visitors with us in the village. They are *Americans*. They are our allies."

There is no response to this news, so she continues, the smile still splitting her face.

"Does anyone know where America is?"

Silence.

The green doors open with a bang and the caretaker bursts through, pushing a large blackboard on wheels.

"Move! *Move!*" he bellows.

He appears to be mowing down any child who can't get out of his way. Mrs Meeks waves him on towards her.

"Thank you, caretaker. Over here with it, if you please."

The blackboard arrives at her side and the caretaker swings it around to reveal a large map pinned on the other side. I can only see the top half.

"America is here."

I see her lean forward, ruler in hand, and then there is much clamour and scrapping as Mrs Meeks and her ruler disappear. The caretaker shoves children this way and that, and after some shuffling and scraping, the ruler reappears over the heads of the other children. I can hear her talking — something about an ocean and the Germans — but I can't make any sense of it. I want to know who the Yanks are. I know about America: there are American Indians who fight cowboys, but what have they got to do with the war? Anyway, the men I saw this morning were riding in jeeps, not on horseback. The map remains on the blackboard and at playtime I hang back to have a look at it; it is a confusion of yellows, greens, browns and blues and has lines drawn all over it. Who could understand this? I ask myself as I lean towards it.

"Hey, you! Don't you put your grubby little hands on that!"

With one swipe of his arm the caretaker sends me reeling across the room. I shoot out into the playground. I will have to find out about the Yanks some other way.

At midday I go home. I won't be able to ask Jack anything, as he takes a sandwich to school for his dinner. The wireless is playing in the corner of the room. The news is on. I eat my dinner. "American forces have landed in the British Isles," says the commentator.

"Who are the Americans, Mother?"

"They come from America."

106

This gets me nowhere, so I continue to address the voice from the kitchen.

"Who are the Yanks?"

"They are the Americans."

"So are the Americans and the Yanks the same people?"

At last I am getting somewhere. But when Mother comes into the room, wiping her hands on her apron and pushing her hair out of her face, she says:

"Stop asking so many questions! One day you'll get into trouble with all your questions. Just you leave those Americans, Yanks, or whatever they want to call themselves alone. They'll get on with their work, and we'll get on with ours. Get back to school."

With my coat pulled straight, I am pushed out of the door. But at least I now know who the Yanks are.

That afternoon, when Jack comes home, I am anxious to tell him about the Yanks, but he replies with a sneer in his voice:

"I know that. They are the cowboys. They are like Roy Rogers in the films at the picture house."

For a moment I am disappointed. I'm not the first to find out who the Yanks are. But then I remember that I have other news.

"Mother says we should leave them alone but Mrs Meeks likes them. Maybe we are going to fight them."

Jack's reply holds a good deal of contempt and a tinge of triumph.

"No, Dot. They are our *allies*. That means they are our friends."

"Maybe they are going to fight the German prisoners."

Bert, Arthur and George have arrived in the garden, and it is decided, there and then, that when the weather allows, we will investigate the issue of the American soldiers.

So, on Saturday morning after Jack and I have carried the groceries down from the Co-op, all seven of us set off to look for the camp. It is still cold and a strong wind is blowing the clouds across the sky. We walk as quickly as we can to the falling ends. We are eager to be away on our mission, but we don't run in case an adult notices our excitement and questions us.

As soon as we are heading out of the village our freedom is assured. I run hard to keep up with the boys, and before we get to the bottom of the hill I am hot. Bert stops.

"Where do we go now?"

The road runs on before us and disappears out of the village, and a smaller road branches off to our right. Harry is standing at the top of this road, looking up at a board that sticks out of the hedge.

"'Military Establishment.' Look, it's the same place the soldiers chased us from when we were looking for the Germans!" he calls.

The boys are across the road, ready to head off towards the camp. I am reluctant to follow, but I am more reluctant to be left alone, in case the German prisoners are still somewhere near.

"What's it mean?" I ask.

Harry points down the road.

"It means there are soldiers, in the military, in that direction."

I want to remind the boys of the soldiers — and the dogs — we met last time, but they are already off. I pull my pixie-hood over my head and run to catch up. Again it seems that Harry has taken the lead, and now he stops with his hand held up to halt us.

"Shush."

We all stop, colliding into each other as we do so.

Jack asks: "What is it?"

Harry doesn't have an answer. It's just something he senses. So we all kneel on the grass by the road and peer around the corner. Arthur is in front.

"I can't see anyone. We could creep down at the side of the hedge. There aren't any nettles."

So, throwing caution to the wind, we creep by the hedge and in a tight group peer around each part of the wide bend as it unfolds before us.

The large metal gates appear, seemingly nearer than last time. We drop back in a tangled heap. There is a soldier, carrying a rifle, standing right by the gate.

Remembering what happened last time, we have tried to be silent, but our activities have attracted his attention, and now he swings around and looks up the road. All this has happened in a flash and pandemonium breaks out. Bert's feet are in my way, and as I turn to run I fall on to the grass, Arthur trips over my legs, staggering into the hedge, and Mike sits down in the nettles.

In the panic and confusion we don't hear the crunch of boots on the road.

109

"Hi! Are you kids from the village?"

Jack, who has managed to pull himself to standing, speaks for us.

"Yes, sir."

Changing his rifle to the other hand, the soldier lifts Jack's hand and shakes it.

"Well, I'm pleased to meet you, sir."

Jack's face is red. No one has ever called him "sir" before. The man who stands smiling over us is younger than Father. He is slim and tall, and his blue eyes, which show just below his helmet, light up his face. He is still eating his dinner, chewing all the time as he speaks.

"Maybe we will be able to come and see you folks soon."

Jack, who is now feeling well in control of the situation, replies, "Yes, we hope that you will be able to come."

The others aren't so sure and start walking backwards up the road. I try to follow them, but Jack is in my way and I nosedive into the grass again. Reaching down, the soldier picks me up by the arm and stands me on my feet.

"Hey, you guys! Come and look after the little lady here. You're letting her get trampled on."

Someone thinks I'm a lady! My aunts will be pleased. The boys stop in their tracks, growing several inches on the spot. They have heard cowboys in the films call each other "guys", but they have never ever been called "guys" in real life.

Now we are all retreating at full speed. At the top of the road we stop to catch our breath.

"They speak English," I gasp.

"Cowboys talk English and they talk the same as the cowboys do," says Jack.

"Hey, you guys," says Harry, "we'd better get going."

With a great whoop, the guys set off.

"Come on, little lady," calls Arthur.

At first I quite like this name, but by the time we reach the village I have decided that it separates me from the rest of the gang, so I ask if I can also be called a guy. As I am wearing a pair of Jack's old trousers it is decided that this is acceptable. So I become a guy and seven guys race back up to our house.

The American soldiers start to come into the village. They bring with them an air of excitement that is new to us. Infectious music, which makes me want to dance, seems to sound from everywhere. Their talking is like music, too, and they talk all the time — to each other, to the people they meet in our village. Father doesn't seem to think any better of them and comments that they are a bit too smooth, smart and self-important for him. When his friend from the mine says that the Americans are overpaid, oversexed and over here, Father laughs loudly. This surprises me, as he has always said that you must give everyone a fair chance and not judge on appearances. Mother says little, but I notice that she no longer wears a piece of old stocking around her hair to hold it up but instead has found a couple of pretty chiffon scarves, along with a long-lost tube of lipstick. I watch as she contorts her face in order to get the colour in the right place.

One afternoon Jack comes home from school in a state of great excitement.

"A boy at school has got some gum from a Yank."

Mother is on to him like a shot. Putting her hand round his head, she redirects him to stand in front of her and, speaking directly into his face, she leaves him in no doubt about her opinion of gum.

"I hope *you* haven't got any." Without waiting for an answer, she continues, "You just leave that stuff alone. You don't know what it is and what it will do to you. I want no more talk about it from any of you, and I don't want any of the stuff in this house. Do you understand me?"

We know not to talk back.

I have heard talk of the gum at school and am desperate to know what it is. Now someone has actually got some, and I want Jack to tell me about it. But with Mother in this mood and the rain falling in the garden, I will have to wait until we're in bed. We play quietly, even Bob knows not to ask any more questions and Jack learns his spellings without being told. But I notice he keeps putting his hand in his pocket.

At last we are lying in our beds. The candle has been blown out and near darkness reigns.

Mother descends the stairs and with a click, the stair-foot door is closed. For a few moments I lie in my bed in the corner of Mother and Father's bedroom. When the silence continues I slide my feet to the linoleum and, hardly touching the floor, I do my usual dance around to the boys' room. Sliding my cold feet into their warm bed, I ask:

"So what's gum?"

Jack points at Bob, who is already asleep.

"Shush."

He slides his hand under his pillow. Although my eyes have now become accustomed to the near darkness of the room, I can hardly distinguish the shape or size of the object that he is holding with such care. I peer close.

"What is it?"

"Gum," he whispers.

He climbs over me and slides down to the floor. I follow him to the window and pulling aside the heavy blackout curtain, we examine the small, white square.

Letting go of the curtain, Jack lifts the piece of gum, and pulling back the torn corner of the paper, he reveals another small white square. I can smell peppermint.

"Is it toffee?"

I let the curtain drop on the outside of us as Jack unpeels the rest of the paper and replies:

"Yes."

I am not much of an expert on sweets, but I am sure this one does not warrant so much attention.

"It's not very big. I could eat that in one minute."

Now Jack gets quite excited. He lifts up the curtain so that I can see it better.

"Oh, but you couldn't. Harry says that once you start to eat it, it lasts for ever — you don't ever finish it."

113

I am just reviewing the square with new interest when Jack's hand closes over it with a snap. There stands Father in his ARP uniform. He has been doing his weekly stint of fire-watching. Miss Brown, a teacher from the public school, fire-watches with him. All the men in the village have offered to do his watch for him, but Mother says he is far too diligent to let others help. It's Miss Brown who noticed that our curtains were open, and Father has come up to check why. Fortunately for us, in the panic the gum has fallen to the floor.

"I had to get some sums finished for school, and Dot was just helping me to check them over."

Jack is quick with the lie; it is a good thing it is dark, as I know his face will be red.

"What's happened, Joe?" Mother's voice calls up the stairs.

"It's all right, Nellie. These two were trying to get some homework finished, and they had the curtain lifted to get some light."

"We mustn't complain when children want to work, must we, Mrs Compton?"

The thought of a teacher in my house sends me back to my own bed at great speed.

With a grunt Father goes down the stairs. I have the distinct feeling that he hasn't believed a word of what we said, but a cup of tea and some adult company are a better option than trying to beat the truth out of us.

As suspected, nothing gets past Father and the next evening he gives us a sound lecture on the evils not

114

only of begging from others but also of chewing gum. Gum, it seems, can damage every part of your inner workings, from stopping you breathing if you inhale it to stopping up your digestive system if you swallow it. I wonder why the Americans have come to fight the Germans, as it appears that most of them will die from gum before they even get going. Father's final warning is directed at Jack. He does not want to hear that he has been asking for gum from the Americans.

So it becomes my mission to approach an American soldier and ask him for gum. As Jack reasons, I haven't been told not to ask for gum; only he can't. I'm up for the challenge and the boys push me down to the falling ends in a box on old pram wheels. They disappear behind a wall and leave me sitting in the cart. I have been told what to say, so I now sit by the fruit shop door, awaiting my chance.

Suddenly there is a crescendo of voices and the strange accent envelops me as feet and legs come out of the fruit shop.

"Whoa! What have we here?"

Here is my chance, I think, and with beating heart I say my piece: "Got any gum, chum?"

A silence follows. I pretend to be smaller than I am, and try not be seen, but the neat trouser legs bend at the knee and the longest body I have ever seen descends to my level. He is like the "Jumping Jack" man in my book. I spend ages trying to work out how he folds up. Now here he is, folding up in real life. After the knees, his hips fold, and then his waist comes down, and now his face is now almost level with mine. A hand comes up and places itself on my arm. I look at it in utter amazement. It is black. That is, it is black until it turns over, and then it is pink. I look up to his face and see the darkest eyes I have ever seen. He also has the biggest smile I have ever seen, with the whitest teeth, which light up his face like a lamp. I have a black doll who, like her pink friends, sits on the top of the hen house. But I never thought that somewhere she must have a mother and a father who, like her, are black. Now, here he is, my black doll's father. I try to tell him this, but nothing comes. Instead in a soft, sing-song, voice, he asks:

"And who, may I ask, are you?"

"Dorothy," I manage to say.

"Then we had better see what we've got for you, Miss Dorothy."

Reaching into his pocket he produces a strip of white paper with a green stripe on it, and holding it out to me, he says:

"There you are, little lady. Now don't you go getting lost."

He starts to go back up again, his head seeming to disappear into the clouds. I watch him as he rises and another black face and two white faces look down at me, wave and walk off.

In seconds I am surrounded. With great speed the boys swing me around and push me — jerkily — up the hill. My mind is full of the man I have just met.

"He was black," I say over my shoulder. But the boys aren't very interested. I have the gum and that is all that matters. I know that people who have black skin live in Africa. The Baptist Chapel runs a missionary service, and I have seen slideshows with pictures of black people dancing. My aunts were very upset that we were allowed to see pictures of ladies without dresses. They told me that we had to go to Africa to save their souls and I asked if we had to teach them to wear clothes. But the man I have just met was very well dressed and I am sure that my aunts would have fully approved of his dress and his very good English. I make a note to ask Aunt Flo if missionaries have been to America.

My thoughts are soon interrupted as the boys swing me on to the waste ground, in front of the Old Mill. I hand over the gum. Now that I have got it, it no longer matters to me. But it matters to the boys. One or two pieces have been given out in the village, but we are among the first children to get any. The news spreads fast and it isn't long before a crowd gathers to look, touch and smell it. Everyone wants to know of my act of bravery and endurance in getting the gum. And as the day wears on my feats grow and become mixed up with missionary exploits. The man, with a smile as wide as the new moon, a smart pair of trousers and a soft sing-song voice, becomes a little more ferocious and even does a bit of dancing.

CHAPTER
NINE

They came and they were like us, but they went, to where we knew not

September 1943 — March 1944

Father doesn't soften and instructs us to stay away from the Americans. So when Jack comes home and tells anyone who is listening that an American soldier has asked him if he has a sister, and if so to tell her, "If she wants some nylon stockings meet me at the crossroads at seven this evening," Father almost chokes on his tea. He slams down his mug and heads for the door.

"I told him that she doesn't wear nylons," says Jack but Father doesn't turn back around.

One of the girls at school has an older sister who has been on a date with an American soldier who gave her some nylon stockings. I'm not sure exactly what nylon stockings are. I know that Mother has a pair of silk stockings. Her sister gave them to her for her birthday. Mother says that they're to be worn only on special occasions and I have never seen her wearing them. I have seen her sitting alone in the bedroom pulling the stockings over her fingers and looking at her hands

118

through them. Once I heard her sigh and when she saw me, she put the stockings back in their packet and pulled me towards her, tightened the ribbons on my plaits and pushed me out of the room. She always wears lisle stockings — sometimes thick ones, sometimes thin ones. When she wears no stockings, because it's hot — which is hardly ever — Father tells her it is "not as hot as it is in hell", which I don't understand.

I don't hear any more about my invitation to meet the American soldier. We get used to seeing them around the village and I always say "Hi" whenever I see one.

One Sunday morning, I am lying straight and still in my warm bed, listening to the sparrows chirrup outside the open window. Their one-note song has been ringing out since the first ray of sunlight. It sounds free like Sunday morning with school and shopping forgotten, clean like the clean billow of my freshly washed hair which lies beside me on the pillow and fresh like the freshness of Sunday best clothes. The smell of frying bacon drifts in through the window from next door. We don't have bacon in our house, but the thought of my breakfast makes me feel very hungry. On Thursdays, Mother cooks a few pieces of stewing steak and for all of Friday it sits in a mixing bowl with one of her flat irons on top, pressing it in readiness for Saturday tea. She always saves Father a piece of the meat for his weekend breakfast and on Sunday mornings we

119

children have the gravy on thick slices of bread with a sprinkle of salt.

I lift my head and look across the room. Mother is still in bed, her head down among the blankets. But Father is gone, probably doing one of his half-shifts. Mother turns over, her eyes still closed, and I take the moment to look at her. Her health isn't very good, but she always works herself hard. She makes us work hard too. Not only must we be clean; we must always be top of the class. "Second place is for someone else," she tells us.

Mother stirs. Her voice is full of sleep, but it makes me start.

"Are you all right, Dorothy?"

"Yes, I was just listening to those noisy sparrows."

Her eyes watch me over the blankets. I always feel that she knows exactly what I am thinking. She has those clever kind of eyes, the sort that seem to look through you and confuse you. But somehow she never seems to come close to me. I never know what she is thinking.

She sits up, her brown hair over one side of her face, and for a moment I see the beautiful young woman in the picture — but only for one moment: the look of concern is quick to rise.

"Better get up and get moving. Your father has invited some soldiers for tea today."

It takes some moments for the words to sink in.

"American soldiers?"

Bob patters across the bare linoleum floor. Mother swings him off his feet and carries him down to the

120

kitchen. As I get myself dressed, I shout into Jack and Bob's room.

"Jack, get up! Some soldiers are coming here for tea!"

Jack almost knocks me over as he tumbles down the stairs, three steps at a time.

"*American* soldiers? Coming *here*?"

Steam is rising from hot gravy. We sit down at the table and for a few moments concentrate on soaking the gravy into thick slices of bread. But as soon as we are finished, we are buzzing with questions, Jack and I imploring Mother to tell all. But she silences us. She is not looking at us, which means she doesn't want the conversation to continue.

Bob, not yet five, hasn't worked this out yet. So he asks:

"Does Father know they are coming?"

"Of course he does," she snaps. "He invited them. *Americans*, here, in our house. Goodness knows what I am going to give them to eat."

As if to say "this is all I've got to give them", she gathers up the crumbs from the bread and puts them back on the top of the loaf. She orders us off to Sunday school.

It is a mystery to me that we have to go to Chapel with Aunt Betty and Aunt Flo and that Mother never comes. Every Sunday I pray she might change her mind and come with us the week after, but it never happens. I want her to dress up like all my aunts and come with us. It would make her proud to see how well behaved we are when we come in to the service at the end of Sunday school.

"And keep clean," she shouts out as we leave.

We walk up the road, Bob dancing at our side.

"What do you think has happened?" Jack asks.

"I don't know, but I suppose if they are coming to tea Father can't be too angry with them."

I say this without conviction, because I can't think what has happened to change Father's mind so dramatically.

Sunday school passes and we return home, clean. The beautiful smell of a Sunday roast fills the living room. Even though it is only stuffed cow's heart, Mother can make it smell good. As soon as we have eaten, Mother leaves the table, goes into the pantry and fetches the mixing bowl. Father takes the large kettle into the kitchen and putting a little soft soap into the bowl, pours hot water on to it and begins to wash the pots. Father usually washes the pots, as he says it keeps his hands clean, and usually we have to be coerced or threatened into wiping. But not today. Today we want information. Jack stands close to Father, and as he passes over a plate he asks, as casually as he can:

"Do you know these American soldiers, Father?"

Pushing the plate at him, Father's reply is abrupt.

"Of course I do." Then, after washing another plate, he mumbles, "Well, I think I do."

Bob is feeling brave. "Well, aren't you sure?" he chirps.

"I met this bloke in the Black Boy last night, who ended up buying me a pint. He was a nice bloke. His name was Alvin, or something like that. Said he was a miner in America. He said the job suited him because he was already black all over. We had a good laugh."

"Is he the one who is coming?" I ask.

"I think so. He had a couple of blokes with him. I don't know if they are coming as well."

"I met a black soldier at the falling ends. Do you think it's the same one who is coming?"

Father has turned over the bowl in the sink and is now wiping his hands.

"Don't know, Dolly. There were quite a few in the pub last night. We'll know who he is when he gets here, won't we?"

Mother sets about things with gusto and soon one of our favourite treats is coming out of the oven. Claiming the last of our homemade jam, a fine Victoria sponge cake stands proudly on the table. There is tea in the pot and anticipation in the air.

At three o'clock on the dot, a knock sounds on the kitchen door. We three children stand in a row; Mother stands beside us, wearing her best, flowered dress, a chiffon scarf and red lipstick.

Father answers the door.

"Do come in," he says in a friendly voice.

Father's smile tells us it is Alvin, whom he met in the pub. Two younger men follow him. The kitchen feels crowded. I have always thought that our house is quite large, but now it is suddenly small. One of the young men is very tall. In fact, he is so tall that he has to bend his head in order to stand in the kitchen. He stands by the open door. Like the man whom I had met at the falling ends, he is very black and his dark eyes shine in the dull light of the kitchen. The other man is just a little shorter. He has a very pale face and hair that is as yellow as ripe corn. He stands with his back pressed against the sink.

The curtain between the two rooms has been pulled to one side and Mother positions us in a line across the living room as she extends her hand towards Alvin.

"Do come in."

Alvin steps forward, watching Mother's face from under the peak of his cap. Then he takes off his cap and places it under his arm. He takes her hand.

"I'm delighted to meet you, Mama, and thank you very much for inviting us to your lovely home."

Blushing with pleasure, Mother nods her thanks. For one moment the beautiful, young woman appears again as she smiles at her visitor.

"I wonder, Mama, if you could relieve me of these? They are weighing rather heavily in my pocket."

Alvin has something golden-coloured in his hand and is offering it to Mother. For a moment she looks at him in disbelief. Then in a reverent tone she whispers:

"Cling peaches."

"From the people of America. Only wish we could get more to you."

With one look, Mother embraces the whole American nation, and taking the tin and holding it as one would imagine a crown is held, she calls out:

"Joe, open these, will you? We'll have them for tea."

Alvin's white teeth shine as he smiles at Mother.

"No, Mama, these are for you. Save them to eat on some special occasion."

Mother hesitates for a moment, opens her mouth as if to say something, closes it, smiles and places the tin on the top of Father's wireless. We look on in shock. The wireless is Father's most treasured possession and nothing is allowed in its space. But there the peaches stand.

Mother's shocks are not yet over. The young man with the yellow hair produces a cellophane packet and turning to Father, says: "May I offer this present to your wife, sir?"

Father stares at the front of the packet — where ladies legs curve gracefully one over the other — and is at a loss for words. Alvin steps in to the rescue.

"These are from the women of America, Joe. I think my wife would kill for a pair of these. We should get the American and German women to fight it out over a dozen pairs of nylons and then we men could go home."

He is laughing as he says this and suddenly all formalities are gone. Mother becomes Nellie and Jack, Bob and I are each given a bar of candy. The candy and stockings join the peaches on the wireless. The two young men are introduced as Pete and Elmer, and Father and Alvin retire to the kitchen. Alvin produces two cigars and they settle down to talk.

Elmer smiles down at us.

"You play baseball?" he asks.

At least that's what we think he asks, and when he pulls a grey ball from his pocket, we settle for this

125

assumption. Jack is looking at the ball but I am transfixed by Elmer's face. I have never before seen such beautiful-coloured hair and such green eyes, and now I see that he has a moustache and everything about him looks golden. Feeling my gaze, he turns towards me. I smile back and then look away.

"I don't think we play baseball," says Jack.

Elmer throws the ball over to Jack.

"Here you are."

But Mother doesn't like ball-throwing in the house.

"If you are going to throw a ball," she says, more kindly than usual, "you can go into the garden."

We take the two Americans into the garden and in the warm afternoon sun we throw the ball around to each other on our small lawn. Pete has enormous hands and he never seems to miss a catch. It is very hard for me to throw to him, as I have to throw the ball right up into the air.

Elmer says: "This is how you pitch."

He swings his right arm behind his head, lifts his leg and flings the grey ball forward. It whizzes through the air, thumps into the side of the hen house and rebounds across Aunt Lily's garden. The hens run in all directions, squawking loudly. Mother comes to the door and even though she doesn't say anything, Elmer quickly recovers the ball and puts it back in his pocket.

I want to carry on playing.

"We can show you how to play cricket," I suggest.

We have a small cricket bat and a tennis ball. Pete looks odd when he tries to get the bat in the crease, as he almost has his head on the ground, and when Jack bowls, he returns to baseball and the tennis ball is last seen disappearing over the hedge at the bottom of the garden.

The five of us look for the ball. Pete and Elmer can see over the hedge, while Jack, Bob and I look through it. But the ball is lost — no sign of it, just rows and rows of small cabbages and lots of weeds. We are rescued by the Victoria sponge cake.

Mother's voice is almost singing as she calls: "Does anyone want a piece of cake?"

The soldiers don't move but we shout in chorus: "Yes, please!"

The best china is on the table, the cake is sitting resplendent on the glass cake dish and biscuits have been retrieved from some hiding place. The chatter is loud as tea is drunk and cake is eaten. Now we can certainly understand each other.

But all too soon Alvin rises and looking at his large wristwatch, says:

"Well, I am sorry to say we had better be getting back to camp."

All three are filling the kitchen again. Father has his hand shaken; Mother's hand is held for some time; promises are made to return for more delicious cake. Jack's hand is shaken, Bob and I are hugged. Elmer even kisses my cheek, his moustache tickly.

Now all is quiet and they are gone.

"Nice boys, aren't they?" says Father as he carries the clean china back into the houseplace. Mother's eyes rest on the peaches, stockings and candy. With her hand across her mouth she walks towards them. Touching them with two fingers, she sighs.

"I don't know. I've never seen so much for years." A tear escapes and pushing it aside, she murmurs: "What a shame we have to meet such people in this way! We should be able to get to know them. They seem to be such easy people to like."

Father puts his arm around her.

"Maybe when this is over we will be able to go over to their country."

I stand by the door, watching them.

"Well, maybe Dolly will go. I think she took quite a shine to Elmer."

Father is laughing and touching my blushing cheek. I head down the garden to the boys.

Later that night, when Father is tucking in my blankets, I ask:

"Will Pete and Elmer come again? They want to learn to play cricket and we didn't have time to teach them."

"I'm sure they will if they can, but they might soon have to go away to fight."

"Where will they go?" I ask.

"I don't know. They aren't ours. I don't know where they will be sent, but no doubt it will be to some bloody front."

In the half-light of the room I watch my father as he stands and stares out of the window.

It is some time before Mother looks at the nylon stockings, even though half the village have been in to peer at the cling peaches on top of the wireless. I arrive home from school and she has the packet on the table. I can tell they have been opened, as they are folded back in a different way.

"Do you want to have a look at these stockings?"

Without waiting for me to reply, she removes them from their packet again. The picture of the legs becomes white and she lays the stockings on the table. I look at the two flimsy legs as they lie exposed.

"How do you put them on?"

She lifts one stocking, curls the finger ends of her right hand into the palm and slides her fist into the stocking. With a sigh, she replies:

"With great care."

She gazes at her hand, transformed by the delicate material. Then, looking into my face, she smiles.

"As with most things that have to do with being a woman, you handle them with great care, Dorothy."

The American soldiers stay in the village for the winter — dark nights and blackouts and heavy, woollen coats and snow. One of the branches of the ash tree appears to have fallen.

Mother and I examine its trunk as we stand by the paper shop door.

"That branch never fell off," she tells me. "You can see where it has been cut."

Father tells us the story that is going around the village. One night old Mrs Aslope, who lives in one of the tumbledown houses at the back of the paper shop, had got her son to climb up the tree and cut off the branch. Father says he hopes she was able to keep warm. "Warm for a couple of weeks, anyway," he says sadly.

We don't see Alvin or Pete or Elmer again. The village is so full up with American soldiers that at times it feels that there is hardly room to get your feet on the pavements. But we don't mind. They have brought something that we have not known before, a sunlight and brightness in contrast to our dark and austere winter.

But we wake up one day and they are not there. The village stands as empty as a field when the fair has moved on.

CHAPTER
TEN

We knew the face of one who died

June 1944

"It's my birthday soon."

I announce this to anyone who is listening, but no one is.

I tell the team as we gather in our garden on Saturday afternoon.

"It's my birthday in two weeks."

Bert is always eager to get an invitation to food.

"Are we coming to your house for tea?"

"I don't know. I keep reminding Mother, but she's ignoring me."

The weather is fine and as May wears on, the days grow long. When not at school I spend much of my time queuing for food and playing on the recreation ground. When not working, the adults spend much of their time listening to the wireless and talking in small groups. There seems to be something in the air, unspoken words hanging above our heads.

"Can I have some red shoes for my birthday?" I ask.

I have been to a tap-dancing class at school and I want to go again. But the teacher says I can only go if

I have tap-dancing shoes — red with bars across the front and white ribbons to hold them on. At the class, a girl, who lives just out of the village, told me that she is to have these shoes for her birthday present. She has a picture of them and shows it to everyone. These are the shoes I want: shiny and red and bright, they are fixed in my imagination and almost daily I remind one parent or another that I want red shoes for my birthday.

"You shall have red shoes," replies Father.

"Don't fuss, Dorothy. We shall see," says Mother.

But no one asks me what these shoes should look like.

Mother and Father seem to be in a faraway state of mind.

It is Wednesday evening. Father puts on the radio as soon as he has taken off his boots. At first the sound is quite loud, but then it starts to fade. Grunting to himself, Father starts to twiddle the knobs on its front and then he hits it on its top with his fist.

"I reckon we've got a dud battery. This one hasn't lasted for a week."

He speaks to no one in particular, but we all know what Father's mood will be if his wireless won't work.

"Put it in the oven for half an hour while you get changed," suggests Mother.

Father unscrews the wires that hold the battery in place and lifts out the large glass box with red and black knobs on top. Mother opens the oven door and Father carefully places the box on the bottom shelf. Leaving the door open and mumbling to himself about having to go round to Bill next door, to find out what is happening, Father disappears.

I look over the fireguard at the glass box. I know this is the battery that makes the wireless go. I know that I must not touch it unless it is standing in its large metal frame with a rubber-covered handle. On Friday evenings, after school, Jack and I carry the battery up to Speed's Garage. We stand in a long queue, mainly of other children, who are also carrying a battery. Holding our breath against the horrible smell, we place our battery on the floor by the counter.

"Don't spill the acid on your legs," says Mr Speed as he takes our three pennies.

The battery is heavy, the job is hard but we do it with pleasure because we love listening to Uncle Mack — in real life Wilfred Pickles — who tells us the stories on the wireless on *Children's Hour*.

On Saturday, when the battery is charged up to the hilt, Mother takes her few weekly hours of rest. As soon as Father has gone "up for a pint" and we are in bed, Mother — armed with a quarter-pound of sweets — puts her feet up and listens to classical music and the stories of "The Man in Black". Nobody can interrupt her during this time.

But today is only Wednesday and the wireless has been playing for so long each evening that the charge in the battery is almost finished. We will need to find some money to get it charged at Mr Speed's. How will there ever be anything left to buy me a birthday present?

I begin to feel quite concerned. This birthday is not being taken seriously.

"Be quiet and be good for a while," instructs Mother.

"Can I ask June to come for tea for my birthday?"

"Shush," she replies, putting her head nearer to the radio.

Some friends usually come to tea on birthdays — Bert and Arthur and maybe one other friend. As my birthday is in the summer, we usually carry the table out and sit in the garden to eat, but as it approaches this time, my parents appear to become more and more preoccupied.

"They've forgotten my birthday," I tell Jack.

"I thought you were getting some red shoes," he replies.

I thought I was too, but Mother's gone quiet. I don't know if I can even have anyone to tea. Jack can't make sense of things either.

The day before my birthday is a school day. I come downstairs to see Mother sitting in her nightdress listening to the wireless. Before I can speak, she puts her finger across her lips. We listen to the newsreader.

"Yesterday, Allied forces landed on the Normandy coast and it has been verified that a bridgehead has been established."

For a moment I think Mother is going to fall. With her hands to her face she rocks forward as if under some great emotional force. At almost the same moment the back door bursts open and Bill, from next door but one, is in the room. His mouth, wide open in a triumphant roar, looks pink and enormous in a face black with coal dust. He picks Mother up and swings her around. Then seeing me, he picks me up, swings me around and throws me into the air. If he had thrown me straight I would have hit the ceiling, but as I am thrown sideways, I narrowly miss it.

"They've done it, they've gone and bloody done it," he shouts as his wife, also in her nightdress, comes through the door.

"Where's Joe?" Bill asks.

"Still at work, Bill," replies Mother.

Picking me up again, he whirls me around, and putting his hand in his pocket, he hands me some coins.

"Those are for your birthday — a happy one, I hope."

"It's not my birthday today," I try to say, but he has gone.

Still wearing her nightdress, Mother follows Bill's wife into the garden. Breakfast is ignored and as we follow Mother into the garden, we are ignored.

"What's happened?"

But there is no answer. Jack and I take ourselves off to school.

Everything is different. Even the village is upside down. Elderly ladies who usually walk slowly with their heads bent are hurrying along the pavements, stopping to speak to the elderly gentlemen whom they are used to ignoring. The delivery woman stands by her van, a smile on her face as she talks to a miner who still wears

135

his pit dirt. Bert and Arthur's mother stands at the door, talking to her neighbour.

Things become a bit clearer at school, where Mrs Meeks tell us that English and American soldiers have crossed the English Channel and landed in France. I know this is good, but I am cross that they are messing up my birthday. I haven't had a straight word out of any adult about my red shoes or about who will come to tea.

No one seems to take any notice of us children all morning and at dinnertime Mother is still glued to the wireless. She doesn't appear to have moved when I return home after school to find her and Father hunched forward, loud shushes on their lips. We can't help but listen.

"Losses have been substantial."

And a few moments later:

"Losses are not reported as heavy."

"Are we winning now?" Jack asks.

"Well, we've not won yet," replies Father. "But the boys have got their feet on French soil and they're dug in. So we stand a chance now, although it seems we've lost a few."

I can't understand where or how they have got lost. I don't dare ask.

"Yes," continues Father in answer to a question Jack has whispered, "it will be the same boys who marched through the village and the same American soldiers who stayed here."

"Have many been killed?" Jack asks and even Bob is silent as he waits for Father's answer.

136

"I think so," replies Father.

We go to bed. There is no sunlight on the windows tonight. The room is dark. It has been a dark day.

"Is the war over?" I call into the shadows.

For a moment there is silence.

"I don't think so," says Jack. "My teacher says he thinks that we have been making plans to land in France for some time, but the weather has been too bad. He says that we are now taking the war to the Germans."

"What does that mean?"

"I think it means we have gone over to France to fight the Germans."

The stair-foot door creaks.

"Go to sleep, you two, before you wake Bob," says Father.

The next day is my birthday. When I come downstairs, there is a pair of red shoes on the table. Mother and Father smile broadly when I thank them. I hide my disappointment well. The shoes are dark red, ordinary, with bar straps and buttons, not the red, shiny, tap-dancing shoes of my dreams. Mother tells me that she saw them in a shop window in the nearby town and the shopkeeper went to all the trouble of sending to the factory for them, as he did not have my size in the shop. I decide there and then that even though my red shoes are a bitter disappointment to me, I must wear them with pride. They have cost Mother a great deal of time and effort, and all her spare clothing coupons.

The sun shines on and off all day. When I get home from school the table is in the yard and Mother's white cloth covers it.

"Am I having a party?" I shout as I run through the houseplace.

Mother is by the sink.

"If you don't make me drop this jelly you might have one."

The red jelly, just out of its mould, stands wobbling on the copper top. A plate of fairy cakes with hundreds and thousands shining on their tops stands beside it. Without turning, Mother calls:

"Bob, go down to meet Bert and Arthur from school and tell them to come for tea. Tell Jack to hurry home."

Bob, who has followed me into the house, claps his hands above his head and is gone.

"Dorothy, put the plates around the table. I will see if I can find some cream to put on this jelly."

Mother's voice fades as she disappears down the steps and into the pantry. A large jug of milk has been standing there all day and a thick layer of cream will have settled on its top. This is going to be a great party. As jam sandwiches and Spam sandwiches are placed on the table, Father arrives home. He comes into the yard and kisses me on the head as he joins in the "Happy Birthday" chorus. But he is only there for a few minutes, as he goes in to talk to Mother, their voices tight as they talk quietly in the corner by the wireless.

Mother meets me at the door when I come home from school. It is several weeks since my birthday.

138

"Stay in the house with Bob and tell Jack to stay in when he gets home."

She pulls her coat on and goes. I am confused. Mother never leaves as we are coming home. I go into the garden to see if Bob knows what is going on.

"What's happened?"

Bob is running on the path. I have to stop his game to get an answer. I hang on to his arm.

"What's happened about what?" he asks.

Jack comes home and I tell him we have to stay with Bob. He asks Bob if he knows anything but he just replies that he is hungry. We change from our school clothes and as there is no sign of a meal, we invade the pantry, walking into its cold, dark depths. We dip our fingers into an open tin of condensed milk, cut a very thin slice of bread from a loaf and eat it wandering around the garden.

After what feels like a long, long time Mother returns. We greet her, dancing around for information and attention, but she gives us neither. She takes off her coat, puts a pan on the fire and starts to peel potatoes.

"Set the table."

Still she does not look at us and as she turns to put the chipped potatoes into the pan, I see that her eyes are red and puffy. I want to ask what has happened but I know that I must wait for her to tell us. We eat our eggs and chips in silence. Then, still without looking at us, she says:

"Bert and Arthur's father is dead."

"How do you know?" Bob's mouth is full of chips and food sprays out as he speaks.

"Mrs Baker got a telegram this morning. He was killed in active service, in the landings probably — they didn't say. I wish your father would come home. I hope he isn't going to be late tonight."

She looks up at the large railway clock.

"I'm going back down to sit with Evelyn."

She gets up and leaves the table.

"Clear up the table. If your father comes in before I get back, tell him where I am."

The door closes behind her and she is gone. The clock ticks and we sit, silent. For a moment I am lifted with relief. It isn't my father who is dead. I have a great desire to see him, to hug him, to hear him speak, to see his face. Then, as I silently gather up the dirty plates, I begin to realise what the words must mean to Arthur and Bert. They must want to hug and hold their father, to see him smile at them, to see his face. But they will never be able to again. The enormity of it seems too great to bear. Tears well up and fill the whole of me. It is a meaningless confusion. Mr Baker is dead. I look at the backs of my brothers as they carry the remains of our meal into the kitchen. There seems to be nothing to say, so again silence reigns as we wash the pots in cold water and pile them at the side of the sink.

We go back out into the garden.

"I wonder how Bert and Arthur are," Jack mumbles to himself, not really looking for an answer.

He kicks soil back into a hole — the hole that the five of us had been digging the evening before and which was to have been finished this evening. We wait for the sound of Father coming home, but he doesn't come.

Instead Mother returns and without speaking carries the kettle into the kitchen and re-washes the pots.

"Our father's not dead, is he?" asks Bob.

"No, he'll be home from work soon, so get off to bed before he gets here."

She looks at the clock again and wiping her hands on her apron, she busies herself with straightening the room.

We crawl into our beds. Silence hangs in the dusk; words strain to leap out but can find no form.

Then Bob says: "Won't he come home, then?"

"No," whispers Jack.

"Why did he die?"

"I suppose they shot him."

Jack's reply sounds almost matter-of-fact, as though the death of a father happens every day.

"Who shot him?"

Bob's voice is getting louder and I can picture him sitting up demanding answers.

"Was their father a bad man? What did he do?"

I want to run round to the warmth and comfort of the boys' bed, but I know I can't. Mother has silently drawn the lines — no questions, no answers, no talking. Just the one fact: Bert and Arthur's father is dead.

"I don't think he was a bad man, Bob," says Jack, gently. "They just shot him, or something, when he landed in Normandy."

"Why did they do that?" asks Bob.

"Don't know. They just did it. It's on the newsreels: they shoot us and we shoot them."

"Maybe he'll come back in a bit. Then Arthur and Bert can have their father back."

Thoughts whirl through my mind. I hear Father come home and him and Mother talking in the kitchen. I am getting woozy with sleep but as the stair-foot door clicks and Father's steady tread sounds on the stairs, I make myself stay awake. I watch, under almost closed lids, as he looks down at me, kisses his fingertips and brushes my forehead. I want to leap up and hug him, but knowing that would be frowned on, I lie and let tears roll into my pillow: tears of joy for me and tears of sadness for Bert and Arthur.

The twins stay home from school for a few days. Mother spends a great deal of time at Mrs Baker's house. I hear her tell Grandma Compton that she has taken the news very badly. I can't think how else you might take such news. Arthur and Bert's sister, Beryl — who works in a munitions factory — has to come home to look after them.

A few days later the twins come to play in the garden. They look pale and Bert looks a little thinner. We stand around the hen house. It's difficult to think of something to say.

Suddenly Arthur shouts: "We've got to finish this shelter for the hens, my dad said —"

Then he stops and Bert sits down and starts to cry. The door opens and Father, still in his pit dirt, walks down the garden path. Picking Bert up from the garden path, he hugs him tightly. Bert cries even louder. Arthur walks over and Father pulls him to him. I don't know how Mother knows when to bring such things, but she appears from the kitchen with glasses of Welfare orange juice and biscuits to help soothe their pain.

I had heard a woman at the Co-op saying that the man who used to work there had been killed. Grandma told Mother that the son of her relative, who lives across the road, is "reported missing". I hope that Grandma has not had a telegram to say that Uncle Jim, Uncle Frank, Auntie Flo or Auntie Mabel are dead or missing.

At Chapel on Sunday the Minister asks us to say the Lord's Prayer for all those missing and dead. This is followed by two minutes' silence. Bert and Arthur don't come to our Chapel, so I remember as many words as I can of the prayer and say them for their father.

CHAPTER
ELEVEN

A thousand rats to die

September 1944

Father is dressed in his black jacket and pinstriped trousers. This is a surprise, as it is quite early in the morning and it is a work day. Mother is brushing away at the back of his coat and Father is trying to knot his tie, while looking in the mirror over the kitchen sink.

"Will you leave the coat alone, Nellie? It will be worn away if you don't stop brushing."

He tries to move, but she follows him and starts on the coat sleeve.

"Where are you going? What's happened?"

I stand on the cold, stone floor, aware of my bare feet.

"Nothing has happened."

He pecks Mother's cheek, pats my head and steps out of the back door.

The door closes and he is gone. Jack and Bob stand behind me.

"What's the matter?

Jack has not seen Father leave, so knows nothing about the black jacket.

"Your father's gone to a meeting in town."

Mother pushes us into the living room while Jack continues to claim his right to a straight answer.

"What sort of meeting?"

"Oh! If you must know he's gone to one of his old Union meetings. He's got to go a long way on the bus and then he has to catch a train. I hope they give him his fare money back. If they don't, we'll have nothing to eat this week."

"I suppose going on a train costs a great deal of money," I say.

"Hum."

"Will he be gone for a long time?" I ask.

"No, he'll be back before you go to bed tonight, I hope."

But when we return home from school, Father isn't home. Mother looks at the railway clock every few minutes and her brow gathers. She has tuned in to the wireless several times since we came in. There is news of heavy bombing in Sheffield.

Tea is over, the clock still ticks and Father steps in. Mother leaps up. My heart thrums with relief.

"I wondered what had happened to you."

She doesn't look at him, but brushes past to take pots into the kitchen, speaking as she goes.

"How did it go? There was daytime bombing. Were you in it? Have you had anything to eat?"

She returns and starts removing Father's coat from his shoulders. After glancing at some papers that fall from the pocket, she puts the coat across her arm. Father holds up his hands — as if in surrender — and

145

then, bending forward, he kisses the top of Mother's head and picks up the papers in the same move.

"Which question shall I answer first? Yes, I heard the bombing, but it was not near. Our train was delayed because of it. No, I haven't eaten. Yes, we did a lot of talking — most of it waffle — but we got 'em to talk about safety."

Father retrieves his pipe from the jacket as he speaks and now he sinks into his chair.

"They reckon that we will soon be having youngsters and foreigners starting in the pits."

Mother's voice sounds anxious as she bends over the kettle.

"What sort of foreigners?"

"I don't know, Nellie. Prisoners of war, I think. I don't know how we are going to talk to them, though. Just have to shout, loud, I suppose. They're going to have a foreman on each shift, to deal with all the changes. They wanted me to take that on, but I told 'em I'll stay with the Union. We are going back next month to talk about pithead baths and such things. No more dirty clothes for us at home, hey, Nellie."

Father looks at Mother over the rim of his mug, but she has turned back to the fire as she mumbles:

"Soon have more foreigners in this village than English people." She holds out her hand. "Did they pay your fare?"

"Going to collect it from the pit office tomorrow. I've got a piece of paper signed."

Father produces the paper and passes it to Mother, silver change too. Mother grunts her disapproval as she claims the offerings.

146

Upstairs Father changes his trousers and Mother hangs them back in the wardrobe. Jack and I take our chance to look at the papers on the table. Some of them have the crown on them again, along with the red writing, but the rest are just a lot of typewritten words. We look for the call-up words but can't find them. We put the papers back in the envelope.

The long summer holidays come to an end. I am now in the junior school. In our first assembly Mrs Meeks welcomes us back. She has a job for us.

"We couldn't ask you children to collect iron when we needed that, but now that our country needs paper, we are asking you to collect all the paper you can find. When you have collected some paper, bring it to the school and the caretaker will weigh it. If you collect enough he will give you a badge to pin on the front and you will be a proud member of the Paper Army.

The more paper you bring, the higher up the Army ranks you will climb, from Private, all the way to Field Marshall. All the paper will be collected by the Council, sent to Derby, and recorded for our school. We want to be the champion school because together, we will defeat the enemy."

She holds her fist in the air and we all stand to attention. I am not quite sure what I have to do, but in answer to my country's call, I will do all that is asked of me, to the best of my ability. I stand tall, my head held high. I am ready for anything.

I begin with Grandma.

"Have you got any waste paper?"

I am dancing from foot to foot in my anxiety to get the paper.

"Oh, Dorothy, I don't know if we do. Jack came down yesterday and collected what we had."

Grandma searches in the bottom of the cupboard by the fireplace but can't find anything. Uncle Arthur comes in, wiping his face on a towel.

"What's all this panic to collect newspapers?"

"I want to be in the paper army. I've got to take some paper to school, old newspapers, things that you have finished with. The caretaker will weigh it and when I've collected enough I can get a badge to say that I'm a private in the army."

Jack has been busy, getting way ahead of me. He is already a corporal and as we have to ask the same people, I am finding it difficult to get enough paper to make it into the army.

Uncle Arthur pulls some sheets of paper from behind the cushion on the chair. They have the words "Miners Union" written across the top.

"Will this old rubbish do?" He grins at me.

"I suppose so," I reply.

Back at home, Father looks down at my meagre paper collection.

"Where did these come from?"

"Uncle Arthur gave them to me."

I try to make my voice sound direct, as though I think the act has been made out of kindness. But I know inside me that I shouldn't have taken the papers after Uncle Arthur called them rubbish. I know what they mean to Father, but I am getting desperate.

148

"The bugger won't be so fast at giving away what we gain for him. I suppose he'll be backside-licking for a foreman's job."

My few papers disappear and I have to begin all over again.

"Go and ask Aunt Lily. She might have some," Mother suggests.

I walk around the gardens and knock at my aunt's door. I get the usual telling off for not being tidy, but she produces three newspapers and her next-door neighbour hears me asking and gives me some more paper. When I go to school the next day, the caretaker weighs my collection and by dinnertime, I am the proud owner of a private's badge.

One or two children make it to sergeant's level but even so, my teacher tells us that our school is not doing very well compared to other schools in the country. We need to try harder. When Mrs Meeks sends out a message asking for old magazines and books — "new sources must be found, children" — Mother becomes annoyed.

"Books and magazines? Who does she think we are? I don't have money to spend on such things."

Then I have to stop collecting. Uncle George is missing. Grandma's sister, Great Aunt Joan, has received a telegram. I know what getting a telegram means. The lady in the school playground says it means that a light has gone out, and that it will never shine on you again.

"What happened?" I ask Mother.

"They think Uncle George has been killed. He was in a push in the desert and not many came through it."

"Don't they know if he's dead?" I ask.

There is no reply. Mother washes the cups and I watch her as I wait for the response. It doesn't come. Surely someone would know if he were dead? What happens to people when they die? What do they look like? The prayers we say at Chapel tell us that death is profound and the silence is eternal, but they also say that the soul rises to heaven and returns to life. I have seen dead people on the newsreels, but they are shown lying on the ground. You don't really see what they look like.

The click of Father's bicycle wheels on the kitchen floor breaks through my solemn thoughts.

"I saw Mother at the corner," he says.

Mother turns towards him, hands outstretched, and they stand together, arms around each other.

It takes a long time for Father to settle, but at last he does, and I sit on the arm of his chair. He takes a long draw on his pipe and smoke billows from his mouth and nose, enveloping us both in a perfumed cloud.

"What's happened to Uncle George?"

"He was fighting in the desert. They think he got shot and killed."

I try to make sense of this news.

"But what's a desert?"

"It's a place where there is only yellow, dried sand for miles and miles. It is very, very hot in the desert, hotter than you or I could ever imagine. Uncle George was there because he was a desert rat."

I sit up with a start. A *rat?*

"Was he killed by a rat?" I ask.

"No, he *was* a rat," Father replies.

I jump from the chair arm and run to the back of the room, my head in a whirl.

"I've killed Uncle George," I scream.

Mother comes through the curtain.

"What's the matter with her?"

Father sits forward and looks at me with a frown.

"What are you talking about, Dorothy? Uncle George was in Africa, at the other side of the world."

"Yes, but I made him become a rat and get killed. I made a wish that he would get killed like my baby rats and now he *has* got killed like a rat."

"What *is* she talking about?"

Mother wipes the soapsuds up her arm and returns to the kitchen.

No one seems to understand what I have done. I go down the garden and sit behind the hen house and cry for a long time.

I vow to do everything I can to help with the war effort by stepping up my attempt to collect paper.

Every Sunday — well, as many as I can manage — I visit members of the Chapel to collect money in support of missionary work. These include a lady who lives at the end of a row of tall, thin houses, which lie just past the Co-operative store. There is a garden to the side of her house and one behind it, both of which are full of flowers, and today, as I open the gate at the side of the house and step on to the path, I am overwhelmed by the colour and perfume and sound. It is so beautiful that I am sure this is nearer to heaven than the dark vaults of the Chapel I have just left. I stop by a blue lupin and take one of its small flowers between my fingers, pressing it gently. I have done this so many times before — the flower opens and the ballerina inside wears a yellow petticoat. All the ballerinas on this stem wear yellow petticoats and I know that on the next flower the pink ballerinas wear blue petticoats.

My collection book open at the right page, I tap on the door. Mrs James, who seems so different from her garden, opens at once, as if she has been standing there waiting for me. Her round eyes stare at me through large glasses.

"I've come —"

I start fumbling with my book. But I do not have time to tell her how much I have come to collect.

"You haven't been for two weeks," she says, accusingly. "I can't find money like this, you know. Three pence is a lot of money to me. It might not be much to you, but it is to me. I don't think that I can manage it this week."

If ever I miss a week, she will recite the same complaint, yet she always manages to produce the money from a small, brown purse. This time is no different. Having pushed the money at me with her pointy chin thrust out, she is now about to close the door as abruptly as she opened it. I have to seize my chance.

"Have you got any waste paper?"

The door stays half open and the eyes look at me for what seems a long time.

"Waste! Waste! Waste! What do you want paper for?"

As I explain about school and the war effort, she goes back into the house. She returns, thrusting a few *Chapel Weekly* papers at me.

"Don't have newspapers. I don't believe in having all that rubbish in my house. I get my news from the wireless."

Before I have time to thank her, she shuts the door. But she has given me the confidence to ask and as I press on with my collecting, I manage to get more paper from others on my rounds.

To my great surprise, the next time I visit Mrs James, she doesn't shut the door as soon as she has given me her money. Instead she asks if I am still looking for waste paper.

"Do you take any sort of paper?" she asks.

I'm not sure what other sort of paper there is but I don't want to miss an opportunity.

"Yes, I suppose so."

"Well, you'd better come and have a look at what I've got and see if it will do."

She steps to the side of the door and, putting a hand behind my head, pulls me through. With a click the door closes behind her — the sunlight and garden are gone — and we stand in darkness. For a moment my eyes don't adjust to the change in light. I feel her push past me.

"Well, are you coming?" she asks. "I haven't got all day."

I look through the gloom and see her heading for the flight of dark stairs. The house smells unused, as a wardrobe smells when you open it after it has been closed for a long time. I climb the stairs, scurry along a passageway and then up another, even darker flight of stairs. She stops at the top and holding her head high, she opens a door. Shining particles of dust dance in the air. For a moment she looks into the room, her lips moving in soundless speech as if she is seeking permission from some presence within to enter the room. Then, as though invited, she enters, her head bowed. I stand alone in dusky silence, unsure whether I should follow.

"The paper is in here."

The shafts of light reveal boxes, and large parcels, tied with string, leaning lopsidedly on one another against the far wall. Then I see the books: rows and rows of them, stretching the length of the attic, extending from floor to ceiling. It is the first time that I have seen so many books. We have books at home — five of them, which stand between two wooden elephants on the sideboard, the elephants pushing in an effort to keep the books upright. I once took one of the books to see if I could read it, but Mother ordered me to put it back, warning me that books are not things to play with. There aren't many books at our school. Teachers read to us, giving us little snatches of words, but we aren't allowed to read for ourselves. Now I stand in awe behind this elderly lady, hardly knowing how to move, or how to express my feelings at being in the presence of so many books.

With a sniff and a flick of her glasses, she walks over to one of the bookcases and gently pulling her fingers along them, stands with her head bowed.

"Used to read myself, but these are Harold's books — my late husband Harold's books."

I had never thought of there being a husband, or children, in her life — she just exists on Sundays, after Chapel, waiting behind the door, her small leather purse in hand. I want to join her by the books, to touch them as she has, to take one and to feel it in my hands. But this is her world, and I stand silently.

Turning abruptly, she says, "Well, will these do for your paper?"

The moment is broken like shattered glass. I have no idea what I am being asked; I have no idea what is being offered.

"Will what do?" I ask.

She waves her hand around the room.

"These. Been here a long time, but I'm sure that Harold would be pleased if some use were made of them and I can't think of a better use than the war effort."

For the first time I see her smile and in that smile, I can see that this lady has made a momentous decision. I look at the books. Some, tall and straight, stand in exact rows, some lean at angles against each other. Dusty covers show reds, blues and greens; some are faded beyond recognition; while others, a little broken by use, have pieces of yellow paper sticking out from them. I suddenly see them all as someone's old, beloved friends and I think I should apologise and back away before I disturb them more. But with a swish of movement Mrs James is through the door. I follow behind and as we go back downstairs, she calls to me over her shoulder.

"So when will you collect them? I can't get them down the stairs. You'll have to do that."

We are at the front door now and I want to make sure I have got this right.

"When shall I come back?"

"When you want to move them." With a precise movement, the door closes.

I keep this all to myself during dinner. I don't want Jack getting to the books before me. In the afternoon, when Father has taken a little rest, Bob and I go for a walk with him. I take a deep breath.

"Father, you know that I have to collect paper for the school? Well, I visited Mrs James today, and she showed me all these books, which she has in her attic. She said that I could take them all for the war effort. But I think that some of them are very old and belong to her husband. I don't think I should take them."

My sentence ends in a very small voice.

"So when are you to fetch them?" asks Father. "Did she say that you could have them all?"

"Yes, but do you think that I should take them? I mean —"

My voice falters as Father interrupts me.

"Dorothy, this is a lady of some determination. If she said that you can have them, then she meant it and I'm not going to argue with her. I'd better go up and have a word with her to see what she wants us to do."

"Where have all the books come from?" I ask.

"I think she was a teacher, or some such thing. Her husband spent a lot of time abroad, something to do with mapping. He died quite young — caught some disease or something. Many books, are there?"

So it is that two evenings later Father and I stand at Mrs James's door. True to form, the door is opened the instant we knock and Father receives the same hard stare that Mrs James has given me on so many occasions.

"Good evening, Mrs James. I've called with Dorothy. You kindly said that she could take some paper and —"

Father gets no further. Stepping to one side, she puts her hand behind his shoulder and wafts him through the door. I don't see how she quite does this, but I run behind and follow them up the stairs.

"Are you the man who will be collecting them? They are to go to the war effort, you know. I don't want them being sold by some wastrel."

Suddenly she stops and spins around to face Father.

"You're not one of those rag-and-bone men are you? If you are, you can get out now."

Father backs down the stairs and tries to explain who he is. He pushes me forward.

"I'm Dorothy's father."

She looks down her face at me and for a moment I think she has forgotten who I am. But she hasn't and without saying another word, she leads us to the attic room.

"Don't touch that bookcase over there, but you can take the rest. Let me know when you have finished. Hmm, Dorothy, is it? Sensible name."

With a swish she is gone. I want to say, "See what I mean", but Father is standing in the middle of the almost-dark room.

"Eh, Dolly, quite a job this will be. I think we'd better come back tomorrow evening, early as we can. Better bring some wheelbarrows — and some reinforcements — to move this lot."

The next evening the whole team comes to help. We have two wheelbarrows and our wooden cart. It takes a long time to carry all the books down to the school. The caretaker has been told that we are coming and he is there to weigh the paper and to enter the weight on my card.

A few mornings later, Mrs Meeks stands on her box, smiling from ear to ear.

"Children, we have now been collecting paper for four weeks and I am very pleased to say that our school has collected one of the highest amounts in the country."

One of the teachers starts to clap and we all join in.

"No! No! Don't applaud me. You must save your applause for the girl who has made this possible. Dorothy Compton — who is in the girls' junior school — has collected a great amount of paper. In fact she has collected so much that she has now attained the rank of general. I went to the county office last week to

158

get her badge and I would now like to present this badge to Dorothy herself."

I wanted to share some of the prize with the boys, but Father said that as it was I who found it, it was I who should enjoy it. My teacher leans forward and whispers:

"Go on up, Dorothy. Go on up and collect your badge."

It is the first time that I have been so close to Mrs Meeks — the last time I had only seen her legs through the one eye not covered by my pixie-hood. Now the caretaker is lifting me on to her box and I stand beside her. I look up and see her rouged cheeks and red lips close up. Her fascinatingly neat, grey hair looks like china. Her hand with all its glossy fingernails rests on my shoulder and we stand side by side on the very small box.

"Dorothy, it gives me great pleasure to present you with your general's badge."

Taking the badge from the caretaker's hand — he doesn't smile, he *never* smiles — she turns very slightly and pins it to my long, loose jumper. One of the teachers calls out.

"Three cheers for Dorothy. Hip, hip, hooray! Hip, hip, hooray! Hip, hip, hooray."

The school hip-hips hooray with gusto.

My classmates pull at my jumper throughout the day, all eager to see what a general's badge looks like. Mother says she will make a frame for my badge and put it on the wall. But Father is adamant.

"No, she's got to wear it. We don't get many badges in our part of the world. It's a badge of honour."

Despite being flushed with my achievement, I am still worried about the books.

"But, Father, all those books will be torn up and no one will ever read them again. Don't you think that we could have kept them somewhere?"

"Will you be quiet about the books, Dorothy? If we win this war you can write some more books."

"And if we lose, there will be books for no one," sighs Mother.

"Come on now, Nellie," says Father. "We are going to win. How can we lose when your own daughter is a general?"

Now Mother laughs and pulls me to her.

"Yes, you are right, Joe. We will win. We've got the best."

The next Sunday, when we are coming out of Chapel, a lady comes up to me.

"Are you Dorothy?" she asks kindly.

I nod yes. She puts her hand on my shoulder. The smell of mothballs in her fox fur is quite overpowering.

"Mrs James told me that you have been collecting paper for the war effort. She said that you collected some from her attic. I have quite a few papers that have been in my attic for years. I would like to do my bit, so I wondered if you could arrange for them to be collected. Mrs James said that you were very clean, quiet and polite."

She puts out a hand and pats my face with a snake-like glove.

"So when will you come?"

I speak in my politest voice:

"I will check with my father and let you know."

On Thursday evening Father and I are once again in a dark attic. The lady lives only two doors from Mrs James, so the attics are similar. There is a good amount of paper — maybe even enough to raise my rank to field marshal.

Some weeks later, another letter arrives. It is addressed to Father and has an official-looking stamp on the envelope. As usual, Mother goes pale and silent and refuses to open it. It is put on the mantelpiece to await Father's return from work. He is working all night, so we wait with some anxiety until the next morning.

We listen open-mouthed as he tells us that on a Saturday afternoon in the near future, those children — and their families — who have reached the highest ranks of general and field marshal in the paper-collecting army are invited to the Odeon cinema to collect a special badge.

Father laughs as he swings me around.

"Well, well, our Dorothy is famous."

I am not so sure about being famous.

"What will I have to do?"

"I don't know," replies Mother. "We'll just have to go and find out, won't we?"

Jack is more enthusiastic.

"Maybe they'll give you some money."

He is very keen on getting money these days. Mother gives him a stern look and he makes for the door before the stern words rain down.

Another letter arrives and this time there is an invitation card with it. Mother puts it by the clock, its golden edges gleaming.

I have been to this picture house several times for the children's matinee, but I didn't know that there was a stage and curtains. As I climb the wooden steps at the side of the stage, the soles of my patent leather shoes feel slippery on the wood. I follow a boy around the stiff, red curtain. There is a room hidden behind the curtain in which three children and a man in a brown overall stand waiting. The two boys, who are the oldest, both wear black blazers with badges and coloured braiding, and a girl, of about my age, whose dress is made of frills and lace, has her yellow curls tied up with bright ribbon. I feel drab compared to her, even though I am wearing my best Sunday outfit.

The man puts his hand on my shoulder.

"Right, the young lady is to go first."

He consults his clipboard.

"Are you Rosemary?" he asks me.

I clear my throat, which is now very dry.

"No, I'm Dorothy."

He consults his clipboard again, and then places his hand on the yellow curls.

"Then you go first, miss, and the two young gentlemen will follow."

He stands the three of them in row, the frills first and the blazers second.

"When he calls your name, walk on to the stage. Go right up to the officer and wait for him to pin on your badge. When the audience claps, turn to face them and salute. You must then walk round behind the officer and go off the stage on the other side. Do you understand?"

He is watching the stage as he speaks. A group of girls are skipping off the far side and I realise that the far-off sound, like drums rolling, is the audience applauding. Now I can see the shoulders of a man wearing a navy-blue coat, the intense light shining through his thin hair, making it look like a crown, as it gleams resplendent in its coat of Brylcreem. He speaks, and the audience laugh and then applaud. The man moves to one side and for a moment only bright light fills the space. Then the top half of a very smart, light-coloured uniform appears and I can see the profile of a man, his chiselled features and cropped brown hair standing out against the light. The audience applauds. Hands appear, held up to silence the audience and to direct their attention to our side of the stage.

I stand in frozen silence at the back of the little, dark room.

The man in the brown coat springs into action.

"Are you ready, children? Listen for your name."

In a fluster I step forward. What am I to do?

The man puts his hand on my head and halts my movement. Bending forward, he looks me in the face and asks:

"Are you Dorothy Elizabeth Compton?"

Still bending, he looks at a sheet of paper on his clipboard and then back at me.

"You're our only field marshal, so you will have to go on last. Rather a little girl for such a big task, but you'll have to do the best you can. Orders are orders. Right, then. When you get to the officer, wait for him to pin on your badge. He will then salute you, and you have to salute back."

He stops. The officer's voice is calling and Rosemary, in all her glory, sails on to the stage. I see the swish of white lace as she disappears into the glare of light. The man returns his attention to me.

"When you have saluted the officer and the applause has ended, I want you to go to the microphone and say a few words to the audience. Tell them how you managed to collect so much paper and try to encourage other children to collect more."

Now his attention is back on the other children and the first boy sets off on to the stage.

The man speaks without looking at me.

"Don't start talking until the applause stops, and wait for the officer to lower the microphone for you. Don't say too much — we just need a few words."

His hand is on my back, propelling me forward. I want to flee, to be somewhere else, to turn and run, but I am weighed down. The second boy is on the stage and now only bright lights and a black void face me. The applause dies. The officer speaks into the microphone.

I hear the words: "Field Marshal Dorothy Elizabeth Compton."

The man's hand propels me forward. The officer appears to be at a great distance, yet at the same time menacingly near, as I stumble forward under the momentum of the push. He grows large and when I am just feet away, he swings around to face me, stamps his feet to attention and salutes. The noise and the action together are tremendous, and I am almost overcome by their force. Before I can recover he bends forward, pins a round metal disc, with coloured ribbons, to the front of my dress and steps over to the microphone.

Everything is out of sequence; I have not returned his salute. What do I do now? I frantically try to remember. I become conscious of the microphone; its bulb is now almost at the officer's waist. I hear the audience laugh at his witty comment. Now the microphone and I stand alone, and I can hear the man at the side of the stage hissing:

"Say something, say something."

I haven't really noticed the audience before, but now I see and hear them, and in a dream-like daze, I turn to face the microphone. Someone shouts:

"Well done."

Others follow suit and soon lots of "well done's are in the air. I look out at the sea of faces and then, miraculously, I catch sight of Mother.

Now I know what to do, and with hands folded before me, I smile and bow my head. I thank everyone for helping me to carry the paper. My voice is very small to start with, but it improves when the man in the brown coat comes on to the stage and lowers the microphone even further. As I run out of people to thank, I lower my eyes, and I am just going to turn from the microphone and head for the side of the stage when I remember that all the paper had come from Mr James's books. I tell the audience that a kind lady from Chapel gave me all her dead husband's books.

"These books weighed enough to make me a field marshal," I tell them.

And maybe it is the tension or the thought of death, but suddenly Uncle George's smiling face floats before me. For a moment I look at him, and then I realise what I must confess to all these people.

"I had to collect a lot of paper because my Uncle George was killed like a rat in the desert."

I try to admit that I had killed him, but the audience applaud again and my voice is lost.

Someone shouts, "Bravo," and everyone joins in.

The officer comes across the stage and puts his hand on my head. He bends over to the microphone and his voice booms out.

"How fine it is that a child should cry for her brave uncle, whom she may never see or touch again."

I see Mother smiling and clapping, her hands high in the air. The man in the brown coat comes on to the stage and takes the microphone away. I follow him off the stage. He is smiling and now I smile.

Maybe Uncle George can forgive me again.

CHAPTER
TWELVE

The enemy, my friend

October — December 1944

"There were some men potato-picking today."

Jack's voice is lost inside his muddy coat as Mother peels him out of it. School is closed for a week. We all have a holiday named "Potato-picking Week". Early each morning, all who are able — children and adults alike — climb on lorries at the falling ends and in a medley of singing and shouting are taken to all the farms, where there are potatoes to be lifted from the ground and thrown into sacks.

"What sort of men?" she asks.

"There were six of them. They weren't from around here and a woman said that they were German prisoners and we were not to talk to them."

"And I hope you did as you were told and kept away from them." Mother speaks into his face as it appears.

"Do you think that they were *real* German prisoners?"

Mother snaps. She pushes Jack backwards towards the sink.

"Be quiet, and go and get a wash."

She gives Father a look as he walks into the kitchen. He raises his shoulders and shrugs. Avoiding her eye, he leans on the wall by the pantry door.

"So what *should* we do then, Nellie?" His voice is hard. "Should we let the potatoes rot while young, able-bodied men sit around and do nothing? It's too much for women and children to handle and you know it. It will be raining soon and we'll lose the whole crop."

Her gaze stays on him.

"What, then? We all starve?" he shouts.

But he knows her feelings and that he betrays her, so with his head pulled into his shoulders, he walks out of the house. Mother remains silent, and the frown and anger persist.

It is autumn. The leaves on the ash tree are turning brown and the pavement is covered with keys. The boys are all at secondary school and I am still in the junior school. The team don't meet very often — just an occasional evening on the recreation ground. Now every spare moment is spent queuing for food, gleaning heads of wheat for the hens, or working on the farm. Jack and I have come to the firm conclusion that the men whom we have seen working in the potato field are Germans; and as the season continues, we become used to the men in their grey suits, riding in lorries through the village. They seem to be doing other jobs too and one afternoon I am astonished to see two men in grey jerkin suits mending the roof of the clothes shop. While the Americans were in the village we had forgotten about the shop and our suspicions of its connections with Germany. But now they resurface: how is it that as soon as they come in to the village the Germans are mending the roof of the shop?

When I get home, I tell Mother.

"Yes, I know. Grace told me. They are going to nail her roof back on before it blows off altogether. Are they doing it now?"

Since when has the clothes shop lady become Grace? I didn't know that Mother knew her so well. But then things *are* different. It's strange, because once again I can feel that something is wrong at home — as if a storm is about to burst — but I can't put my finger on why. This time I can't stop myself from asking:

"What's the matter?"

Mother is sharp.

"Nothing's the matter. Go and get out of those school clothes and stop poking your nose in where it's not wanted."

The pastry she is rolling is taking a heavy beating, so I retreat upstairs. Bob comes and sits on my bed. As I struggle into a pair of Jack's old trousers, he asks:

"What's the matter with Mother?"

"I don't know," I reply. "But I'm staying up here for a while."

Before I have time to stay anywhere, Mother's voice calls up:

"Dorothy, come down these stairs and help me, now!"

"I'm just —"

"Stop arguing with me and get down the stairs, now!"

169

I wonder what I have done. Father hasn't joined in, so I can't have done anything too big. I run down the stairs and loyally Bob tumbles down after me. The food is in the oven. Mother is wiping the tabletop, watching her own hand as it whirls across the table. Father is sitting on the settee; just his hands and legs show around his newspaper and he is turning its pages with firm determination. Without speaking. I take the mixing bowl and rolling pin into the kitchen.

"Something's happened," Bob whispers.

The door opens and in comes Jack.

We pull faces at him and nod towards the doorway of the living room.

"What?" he asks.

Before we have time to do any more miming, Mother calls us.

"Come in here, all three of you. Your father has something he wishes to say to you."

Her voice is so angry that an icicle shoots up my spine.

"Oh, Nellie. It's not that bad. You're making a drama over it."

"A drama! A *drama*!"

Turning to us, hands on her hips, face bright red, she forces out the words.

"I'm. To. En. Ter. Tain. A. Ger. Man."

"Oh, come on, Nellie. He's only a boy. He doesn't look much older than Jack."

Father tries to put his arm around Mother's shoulders, but she heads for the kitchen. Her voice holds tears and she spits words with venom.

"I don't care how old he is or how old he looks, Joe. He's a German and you are bringing him into my house. With my children."

Mother's anger frightens me. I watch as she stands by the cold yellow sink, her shoulders rising and falling as she cries. Father stays where he is. I run to the kitchen and put my arms around her middle and my head against her back.

"We'll be all right, Mother. We'll be all right," I whisper.

But she pushes me from her. Wiping her hand across her face, she turns and faces Father.

"Damn you, damn you and bugger all of you and your socialist principles. Have your brotherhood of man! It's just brotherhood when it suits them, murder and destruction when it doesn't."

I have never heard Mother swear and the force of it startles me. Father comes into the kitchen and puts his arm around her shoulders. She tries to shrug him off, but he stays.

"Nellie, Nellie. No need to get so upset. If you don't want him to come, I'll tell him it's off. But this is a frightened, half-starved lad we are talking about here. He hardly knows where he is. I know he's German and I know what they have done, but he's just eighteen, Nellie. He was Jack's age when it all started. Just let him come and say hello; then he can go away."

Mother's voice is muffled against Father's body, but the passion remains.

"How can we talk to him? I don't want that language spoken in my house."

"He speaks lovely English, Nellie, and his manners are fine."

Father holds Mother close to him and for a little while they stand together. When she regains her composure, she pushes herself away from him.

Jack and Bob stay in the kitchen with Mother as Father returns to the fireside. I seize my chance.

"Why is Mother so angry?" I ask as I lean over the fireguard beside him.

"She doesn't like Germans." The words come slowly between puffs of smoke.

"I know she doesn't. Lots of people don't, but Mother is getting very angry. She —"

"Will you be *quiet*, Dorothy! You just can't stop going on, can you?"

His face is hard. I step backwards. No further word is sought, or given.

Now, just as we waited for the American soldiers, we wait once again. This time, though, it is not an ally who is to come through our door, but an enemy, a German. I wonder what he will be like in real life. I have spent my childhood shooting and bombing imaginary Germans. They are the people I have learnt to hate and, above all, fear. Mother's ferocious anger — and dread — spreads across to me as I wait. I visualise every arrogant, violent German soldier I have seen on the film screen, or on newsreel.

He is here.

Father holds the door ajar.

My heart is beating so fast, and I am so afraid, that for a moment I can hardly see him.

"Thank you very much for letting me visit you," says a voice in clear, precise English. "I do apologise if I am imposing on you. I will quite understand if you wish me to leave."

I don't know what Mother is feeling at this moment but she hangs back and just nods her reply. A strained silence hangs in the air. Then Father says:

"Mother, this is Karl Heinz. Karl, this is my wife, Mrs Compton."

He inclines his head towards her.

"Madam."

Mother says nothing as she turns away from him. Now I can see him. He is tall and, like the Americans, he has to bend his head to walk under the doorway to the houseplace. Unlike the Americans, he is thin and his shoulders are rounded. His hair is very fair — almost white — and when Father introduces me to him I expect a triumphant and superior look, but he is pale and tired-looking and his eyes are full of fear and sadness. I had been determined to hold my head high, to be defiant, and to let him know that I am not afraid — that I too can hate. In my mind he has killed Uncle George and Arthur and Bert's father; he has even bombed the cities around us. But now as he stands here, I can see that there is nothing to hate. I can't get a grip on any part of him to hate.

Having been introduced to Jack and Bob, he retreats to Father's side and stands a little way behind him, as if seeking his protection. Father breaks the silence as he pushes Karl ahead of him into the living room.

"Do sit down, Karl. We can't stand here all day, can we?"

Waving his hand at us, Father pushes the kettle on to the fire.

"A cup of tea, I think, Nellie."

I look at my mother. As if uncertain in which direction to move, she remains by the door. I wonder if she is going to leave the house.

"Do you drink tea?"

She does not direct the question at anyone, but rising slightly from his seat, Karl replies:

"My mother takes tea every afternoon. I have always been pleased to join her when I could. Yes, madam, I am very fond of tea."

Mother hesitates. She opens the door of her precious china cabinet and lifts out cups and saucers.

"Do you take milk?"

"No thank you, madam. I will drink it just as it comes, please."

Mother does not look at him — she does not look at anyone. We sit in a row on the settee, cups in hands, Father standing in front of the fire. Karl sits on one of the dining chairs, which has been pulled back from the table, his cup in hand. The clock ticks loudly and the kettle sings.

"Where does your mother live?" asks Mother.

"Our home is in Dresden," Karl replies.

"Beautiful china."

"Indeed, madam."

174

"Is your mother still alive?"

There is silence. Karl stirs his tea — which contains neither milk or sugar — and we sit, not daring to move.

"I have no idea, madam."

Now Mother looks at him for the first time. His chin is up and tears brim in his eyes as he speaks in a voice held firm.

Mother nods and picking up her tea, she drinks it.

Karl stays for about an hour and mostly the boys and Father talk to him. I help Mother clear away the cups and wash them up. It is strange to hear his voice. His English is perfect — it is almost impossible to detect an accent of any kind; his is the voice of the radio commentator, the doctor, the vicar and the schoolteacher. When it is time to go, he comes into the kitchen.

"Goodbye, madam. Thank you for your hospitality."

Mother nods sideways but does not speak, and then they are gone. Nothing is said. Mother puts on the radio and takes up her knitting. Father comes home and still nothing is said.

Later, as he prepares to go down to the Black Boy, Mother speaks into her knitting, her voice sounding a long way off.

"You can tell that young man he can come for a cup of tea next Saturday. That is if he wants to."

Father stops in his tracks, walks over, takes her face in his hands and kisses it.

"Get off, you silly devil," she says, half laughing. "Don't you go expecting me to make some sort of fuss of him. I would hope someone would give my sons

175

shelter if they were lost in a foreign land. I can do that for his mother."

"I'll tell him now," says Father.

Karl is helping the landlady of the Black Boy. That's where he and Father met. Karl was trying to move a barrel but didn't have enough strength, so Father went to his rescue and that is how their friendship began. Father returns to the pub and invites him to come next Saturday, and after that a standing arrangement is set up for him to visit early every Saturday afternoon.

At first I am not too sure about Karl. I am suspicious of his connections to the new poster overlooking the clothes shop. His surname is Heinz and the poster is advertising some food also named Heinz. I commandeer Bert to sit behind the clothes shop with me to see if we can prove a connection.

"We'll watch him as he passes," I say.

"What are we watching for?" asks Bert. "I mean, what do we think he'll do?"

"I don't know. Maybe he'll look across here, and make some sign or something. It's just strange: the first German name I find out about and there it is written above their shop."

As I speak, Karl appears on the far side of the road. It is a cold and windy day; brown leaves from the ash tree are blowing in the air. He is wearing his thin, grey, cotton suit, his hands are dug deep into his pockets, and he is bent against the wind. He takes no notice of the shop, or the poster. All his attention and effort are

176

directed towards getting to my little home. I watch as he passes. I do so want to dislike this person.

"Was that him? Didn't take much notice of anyone, did he?" says Bert. "Can't blame him. It's blinking cold out here. I'm off home."

Bert is on his feet and off across the road. I have to agree with him. Sitting on the ground at the side of the road looking for German spies is too cold a job. Sitting by the fire, looking at a comic, seems more sensible.

"Wait," I shout as I run after Bert. "Have you got any comics to spare?"

He throws open the door of his house and a lovely, warm blast of air hits us.

"Shut the door!" yells Mrs Baker.

She has put on a great deal of weight since her husband was killed. Mother says that she rarely leaves the house, hardly ever goes down to the shops or up to the Co-op.

"Hello, Mrs Baker."

Beryl is hanging wet clothes on to a line over the fire. She peers at me, but doesn't speak.

"What are you after now?"

"Just going to get Dot some comics," Bert replies.

Beryl, Bert and Arthur's sister, stops what she is doing and looks at me.

"You still got Herman coming to your house?"

I don't know what she means. She pushes her face towards me.

"Herman the bloody German," she snarls. "Are you deaf, or just daft?"

I can feel my face turning red.

"His name is Karl."

"I don't care what his bloody name is. Should take the sodding lot out on a field and shoot 'em. That's what they would do to us, if they had a chance. Some people don't know whose side they are on. Well, I know where I stand. They shot my bloody dad, so as far as I'm concerned, we should do the same to them."

Bert has pulled a handful of comics from the cupboard. I grab them, thank him, and telling Mrs Baker that I hope she will soon feel better, I get out of the house as fast as I can.

I stand on the pavement, shaky and tearful. I've never been attacked like that before. I think of Karl. If people feel that way about you, I wonder how much effort it takes just to keep alive? Beryl's hatred is a powerful force and in that moment I know for sure that I will not be able to really hate Karl.

I run up the road, clutching the comics. At home the fire burns bright. Bob is sitting on the rug, Mother is knitting and Karl is sitting upright and straight on the edge of the settee, reading part of a newspaper.

"What have you got there?" Bob asks.

"Comics," I reply.

I throw them down on the settee, and they land beside Karl. He half rises.

"Sorry, am I in your seat?"

"No," I reply, as I turn away, not able to look at him after the harangue, which still rings in my ears.

Bob grabs one of the comics.

"Oh good," he says gleefully. "I haven't read these."

178

"What are they?" Karl asks.

"Comics."

He looks sideways at them.

"May I read one?"

"Help yourself," I reply.

Karl treats the comic with great care, reading each page from top to bottom and then turning the page over and folding it under as he finishes. Bob gets through each comic very quickly and is soon looking for the last one, which Karl still has in his hand.

"You read very quickly."

"He doesn't *read* them," I interject. "He just looks at the pictures."

"I read some of the bubbles," protests Bob.

Karl's eyes move in Mother's direction.

"Would you like me to read one of the stories to you?"

The needles halt their clicking as Mother refers to her knitting pattern. The silence gives unspoken permission and Bob squeezes on the settee on the other side of Karl. I can feel how thin Karl is. Father says he is just a bag of bones.

"Can you read?" I ask.

"Yes, I can read English."

He smiles at me, and probably for the first time I look at him. He has beautiful teeth and incredibly blue eyes. The story begins.

October continues cold. Winter seems to have started early. Winds from the north have blown dark clouds across the sky and the morning light does not arrive.

One Saturday, as I leave for the market, Mother is still in bed. She has been coughing for most of the night. Father is at work and Jack and Bob have gone to the farm. The house feels empty when I close the door behind me.

At Rompton market, the first flurry of snow lands on me as I queue. The women are cold and the stallholders have little food to sell. Rationing is even tighter: all vegetables and fruits are already rationed, the bread supplies are short and for anything edible, the queues are long. It is a cold, frustrating morning, and for all my effort I have little in the shopping bags as I drag them off the bus and up the road towards home.

Mother doesn't come to the door when I arrive. The house is dark and still feels empty, and as I lift the latch and push the door with the shopping bag, I know that something is wrong.

"Mother, are you there?"

Karl comes through the curtain. He puts his hand on my shoulder, stopping me in my tracks.

"Oh, I am pleased to see that you are home, Dorothy. Your mother is ill."

I drop the bag and run through the curtain. The living room is dark and cold, the fire is almost black — just a few yellow flames licking their way through the coals — and I can't see Mother. Karl pushes me towards the settee and as I stumble backwards, losing my balance, panic hits. Mother is lying on the settee, the grey blanket from my bed wrapped around her. She turns her head and holds out a hand towards me.

"Did you manage the shopping?"

Her hand is cold, her face is white and her eyes are closed. Karl stands beside me as with infinite tenderness he takes her hand and places it beneath the blanket. He puts his hand on my shoulder and steers me from the settee.

"I arrived early."

He says this almost as if to explain the whole situation.

"I knocked at the door," he continues, "but no one answered. I looked through the window and I saw your mother's legs, lying by the open curtain. So I came in." His voice catches.

"She was lying on the floor. She was very cold. I thought that she was dead, Dorothy."

He moves his hand quickly across his face and then, with a lift of his chin, he points to the ceiling.

"I hope you don't mind, but I fetched some blankets from the bed."

I look down at the grey blanket. She is so still.

"She's not going to die, is she? Should we fetch the doctor, Karl?"

Mother turns her head from side to side. I put my face on the pillow by hers.

"But I would like a nice cup of tea."

We make the tea. I try to help Mother to sit up, but I can't, so Karl puts his arm around her shoulders and holds her forward. I put pillows behind her.

"Karl, could you please reach my medicine and some aspirins from the cupboard?"

She takes his hand as he gives her the medicine.

181

"Thank you. You are a good lad, Karl."

I have never seen colour in his face before, but now it is red — red right around to his ears — and he looks young, almost like one of the boys at Jack's school.

Mother falls asleep. We put away the groceries, and then sitting side by side on the rug, before the now burning fire, we eat bread and drink the lukewarm tea.

"I hope that it was all right for me to come into your house, and to attend to your mother," Karl says quietly.

"Karl, thank you for coming to the house earlier than normal, and thank you for helping Mother."

For the first time I smile at him.

Mother is not well for most of November. Throughout the month, I return home from the market to find her and Karl sitting and talking in front of the fire.

"You should pay attention to Karl," says Mother. "He was at the university before he got called up. He knows more about our language than most of your teachers."

Karl and I struggle through a few Enid Blyton books together. He is very patient and with his help, reading becomes not only possible but enjoyable.

Winter is really here again and the ash tree is a frozen white. The cold goes right through to our bones. Dashing through from the kitchen to warm ourselves in front of the fire, Bob and I are startled to see Karl in the house. His head is bowed and when he looks up at us, his eyes are red and puffy.

"Hello, Karl," says Bob. "What are you doing here? It's not Saturday yet."

Karl pulls us to him.

"I am pleased you come before I go to leave. I must to go very quickly now."

His English is slightly less than perfect.

"Where are you going? What's happened?"

Bob and I both speak at once, but before Karl can answer Mother comes in, holding a small parcel wrapped in newspaper.

"I wrapped these for you for Christmas, but you had better have them now. Open them. Then you can see if they are all right."

She looks tired and strained, still unwell. Karl takes the parcel, tears welling up in his eyes, and unfolding the paper he takes out a grey scarf and gloves.

"I'm sorry there are so many colours," Mother says.

He looks down at the small multi-grey scarf and the over-large gloves for what seems a long time. When he looks up, tears are running down his face. Mother takes his hands in hers.

"You'll be all right, Karl. You'll be all right. Just keep thinking of your mother and your sisters. I know you will see them again."

Karl remains silent. He folds the scarf and gloves inside his jacket.

"Put them on," says Mother.

"No, I must save them, or maybe they will be stolen from me."

"Here's the picture."

A small round picture is balanced on her first two fingers. Karl takes the tiny picture of her face cut from a larger photograph, looks at it for a moment and then places it in his top pocket and buttons it up. He leans forward and kisses Mother's cheek. His voice is barely audible.

"When I see it, I will be able to see my mother."

He raises his head, turns abruptly and leaves our houseplace. We start to follow him, but with a broken voice Mother calls us back:

"Let him do it alone. Give the lad some dignity," she whispers.

"Where is he going?" I mumble.

"I don't know. They are just moving some of them to somewhere else."

She looks into the fire and after a pause says: "I hope he will be all right."

Later that evening, as I sit at the table struggling with homework, I hear Father say that they have probably been moved to somewhere in Scotland.

"That will be cold; I don't think there is enough of him to survive such cold."

But Father is more confident, or maybe he just wants to reassure Mother.

"He'll make it. He's young."

On Sunday morning there is a ship in a bottle standing on the table. I walk around and around it. I have never seen anything so beautiful.

"Where did this come from?" I ask.

184

Mother walks in from the kitchen and touches the bottle gently with two fingers.

"Your father brought it down from the Black Boy last night. The landlord said that Karl had asked for us to look after it."

There is a small piece of paper by the bottle and Mother looks at it for some time. When she puts it down, I see it has a Christmas tree drawn on it along with the words "Merry Christmas".

The lovely little sailing ship, in its beer bottle, stands on Father's wireless from then on — to be admired but not touched. And to remind us of our enemy.

CHAPTER
THIRTEEN

The last of the Enemy

January — February 1945

"When I was shopping at the Co-op this morning, a woman told me that we can go down to the prisoner-of-war camp."

Mother drops a large enamel dish on to the table, and looking over his paper, Father kicks the black-iron oven door closed with a bang. We fix our eyes on the steaming sago pudding, with its brown cinnamon-flavoured topping.

"Why should we want to go there?" Jack asks.

"Well, this woman says there are still some German prisoners there, and they have made quite a lot of wooden toys and things, and we can go and buy them. Thought we'd go on Saturday afternoon."

We work hard to convince her that Karl will not be there, and Father still wants to know why he should buy anything.

"Who'll get the money if I do part with any?" he asks, to which Mother has no reply.

Nevertheless, here we are, on a cold afternoon, a week before Christmas. We have walked through the iron gates, past the high hawthorn hedge that I crawled

186

through, and as I don't want my parents to think that I know this place, I ask:

"What kind of trees are these?"

"Horse chestnut, I think," Father replies.

"Yes, they are." Jack laughs as he picks up one of the distinctive leaves.

"What's funny about horse chestnut trees?" asks Mother.

"Just thinking how many conkers we've missed," replies Jack.

"I'm beginning to think you've gone mad. You laugh at nothing," says Mother as we walk past the ditch in which I hid. If she only knew. I make sure not to look at Jack.

We stroll past the high wire fence, where the soldier with the dog stood. A notice directs us to walk by the wire fence and to enter a quadrangle formed by four long huts. The quadrangle holds wooden trestle tables, piled with brightly coloured objects. German prisoners stand behind each table — all dressed in the same grey suit that Karl wore. Some of the men wear woollen helmets and most of them hold grey blankets around their shoulders.

There are quite a few people already in the quadrangle, but there is little sound — just an occasional murmur of voices. We wander around the tables. The wooden toys are beautiful — wooden boy dolls with red, blue, green and yellow painted suits as well as girl dolls, dressed in brightly painted dresses. There are wooden snakes, made with parts hinged together; when I pick one up, its head moves and the twist goes all the way down the body. There are wooden trains with carriages behind them, and pictures of smiling people looking out of their windows. Mother and I buy a snake for Jack and a train for Bob — presents to be hidden until Christmas Day.

I turn from the toy trains. Mother has been standing at this table for some time, but my eyes are drawn to the dolls. The man behind the table watches me as I approach. He is even older than Father, I think, and his hair, which shows around his cap, is grey. Like Karl, he is very thin. I point at a boy doll.

"Is that Pinocchio?" I ask.

The man looks at me but doesn't speak.

"I've never seen him," I continue, "but I think that is how he must look."

On the other side of the table the man lowers his body and now looks at me. He smiles and says something I don't understand. His front teeth are brown and broken, and there are lines all the way down his face. He picks up one of the dolls and looks at it.

"Ya. Maybe Pinocchio, but no nose."

As he says this, he pretends to stretch out his own nose. This makes me laugh.

"Maybe he hasn't told a lie yet," I reply.

Raising a finger, the man rubs his eye and to my amazement a tear runs down his cheek. I step back from the table.

"I'm very sorry, I'm sorry," I mumble as I retreat from him.

I find Mother and cling to her arm.

"Do men cry?" I ask as I hang close to her.

188

"Sometimes," she replies. "Why do you ask?"

I tell her about the man and she looks across at him.

"Maybe you reminded him of his little girl at home," she says.

"Do you think he's got a little girl?"

Mother does not reply. She is examining something on the table in front of her. I watch the man as he sells his dolls.

"Do you think his little girl is dead? Do you think he knows that she is dead?"

"I suppose so."

Mother speaks without paying me any attention.

"Have we bombed her? Is she the enemy?"

"I suppose so."

"But how did we know that she was the enemy? How do we know who the enemy is? How do we know where they live? Do we just kill everyone?"

"Will you stop it with your questions?" snaps Mother. "You never stop jabbering."

She moves along to another table and I am left watching the man. He looks across at me and raises his hand slightly to one side. I smile a tight smile and raise my hand a little. I feel ashamed. Suppose we have killed her, suppose he knows, suppose he thinks I am to blame. My face burns in hot shame as I run over to my parents. I examine some plaques with pictures of fields and flowers on them with Father and all the time I dare not look back at the man.

Then we are on our way home, each with something hidden beneath our coat. But not everything is for Christmas. We are given an acrobat to play with. He swings and whirls on two pieces of string stretched between two upright sticks of wood. When I press the bottom of the sticks together he swings over and over.

Christmas comes. We put up the paper garlands and sing our carols in the Chapel, but it's not the same. It still feels as though Karl is missing from our home, as if there is a hole in our family. On Christmas morning the girl doll stands on my table, her dress painted bright red and yellow. As I look at her, I see the man's smiling face and it makes me cry because what if his little girl is alive? She won't have her daddy at home today.

There is little food this Christmas — I haven't been able to get any meat in the market — but as luck would have it, or maybe as the law of nature would have it, Matilda becomes available for Christmas dinner. Two of the hens have already "had to go into the pot". Grandfather says that it is no good keeping the hens when they stop laying eggs, as it costs too much to feed them. Matilda has had two operations, since she insists on putting her head through the wire of the pen and pecking at long pieces of grass. When she swallows these, they get twisted around and become stuck in her neck. She makes the most awful noise and lies on the floor, kicking her legs. Twice Grandfather has removed the grass by plucking feathers from her neck, cutting it open with the sharp blade on his penknife and removing the grass. I assisted the second time, as Father was at work. I had one of Mother's large darning needles threaded with black cotton at the ready and when Grandfather asked for it I passed it to him. I had to hold Matilda with all my strength while he sewed up her neck.

Now Matilda has done it again, but this time it is not possible to remove the grass, as her neck can't be sewn up again.

"We'll have to kill her," pronounces Grandfather. "She'll die anyway."

"I'm not having anything to do with it," says Mother, disappearing into the house. "And I'm not cooking her. Your father will have to do it."

So this time Matilda's squawking and choking ends when she has her neck stretched. Hanging by her legs over the handlebars of his bicycle, Grandfather cycles her back to his house. She returns to the fold on a large plate on Christmas Eve. She is soft and white and warm. Plucked and boiled by one of my aunts, she is accompanied by a sea of chicken soup. On Christmas morning Father pops her into the oven with a few potatoes and onions — "just to brown her up a bit", as he puts it. I think he enjoys talking about what he is doing, as it annoys Mother. His sisters think it is awful that a man should have to cook the dinner and one of them volunteers to come and put Matilda into the oven, but Father bravely waves her aside.

"You women and children go to Chapel and pray. I will master this bird and get her into the oven."

As he says this, he waves a tea towel in front of himself like a bullfighter. Mother doesn't think the idea of a sister-in-law offering to take over her kitchen is in the least bit amusing.

Matilda looks very smart when she returns to the table. Mother serves the vegetables and then leaves. Father reassures us that Matilda wouldn't want it any other way. I feel that I owe her some apology, but I have to agree with Father, and she does go down very well with sprouts and gravy.

The winter continues cold and damp: not much snow, or even frost — just dark days and nights, which seem to run into each other, unbroken by daylight. The raw, wet winds, which blow in continuously from the hills, are unable to dry the pavements and roads. We are very short of food, even though the rain came early this year and Father's hard work means we have some potatoes and turnips. I go to school all week, stand in queues on Saturday and go to Chapel on Sunday. There is little time for play, little time to be free. But late Saturday afternoons are an oasis and I go down to the recreation ground with the rest of the team to join in games of rounders, football and tick-tag. On the many rainy days, when playing on the field isn't possible, we retire to the changing hut and spend time mucking about together, jostling around. The boys push each other into the girls. The girls squeal and protest.

It is a dark wet afternoon and we are confined to the changing hut. An older girl, whom we don't see very often, comes in. She lives at the other end of the village and is not one of my acquaintances.

"Have any of you seen the 'Eyeties' yet?" she asks.

We haven't and we don't know what or who Eyeties are. Questions are thrown at her.

Out of the buzz I gather that there are some new prisoners in the camp, and they are from Italy.

"My sister says they are something else. She's in the Land Army and they've had some of these Eyeties from down the camp. They came to work at the farm, and she says that they are real hot stuff."

I want to ask what hot stuff means, but I think I'd better keep quiet in case they notice me.

"What happened?" asks one of the other girls, who clearly knows the meaning of hot stuff.

"Well, she reckons some of them are real lookers, sun-tanned with 'come to bed' eyes and sort of film-star voices." She mimics the accent. "*You wanta da helpa?* My sister was in the barn, trying to pull some hay down. Well, this Eyetie comes in and asks if she wants some help, so she tells him she wants some hay pulling down. She said he looked her over from top to toe and asked if she wanted anything else pulling down."

Now there is a buzz.

"And before she could do anything he had his hand inside her jerkin. It was a good thing one of the other girls came in, or else goodness knows what would have happened. The next afternoon, well, she had to go out to —"

The crowd moves in closer. My place on its fringe is lost. I try to get my ear in, but don't make it. I never find out what happened, not to her sister anyway.

My Grandfather's sister, Great-aunt Maude, is taken ill this winter, which is of some concern to the village, as she runs the Post Office. My other Great-aunt Lexie, the one with the humming bird hatpin, also works in the Post Office, but Maude is the mainstay. She has been sent to hospital for an operation and is now staying with her husband's sister, who lives some miles away. A woman is co-opted from a post office in a nearby town. She comes to help in the mornings, but returns to the town post office in the afternoon. As we need someone to open up in the afternoons, an Italian prisoner-of-war is conscripted to work in the shop. There is some argument in the village about this, but there is no one else to do the work and apparently he speaks good English. Opinions are divided.

In the Co-op queue, an elderly man thinks it could undermine the war effort having a prisoner run the Post Office.

The woman in front turns around and looks at him.

"Hum, from what I've seen of 'em, they don't want to undermine anything. They're like us. They just want this lot over and done with so they can get back to some proper life. I think they're sorry that fat bugger Mussolini was ever born."

The conversation goes on, but it is my turn to be served and I have to concentrate hard on Mother's shopping list.

Early on Saturday afternoon the sky outside is dark and rain streams down the misty window. I have just returned from a wet morning at the market. Mother has been cooking, and now several loaves and a long slab of caraway seed cake stand to cool. Mother is sitting on the settee and she watches me as I start to pull my coat back on. It's still damp, but I know this look and I try to move quickly, anxious to leave before it is too late. But I am too late.

"Where do you think you're going?"

I try to sound casual as I watch her face out of the corner of my eye.

"I'm going to call for June."

June lives in a large house just out of the village. We go to school together. She doesn't go to the recreation ground because her mother says the children who play there are vulgar. June has a bedroom and a record player. Her mother wears make-up and modern, smart clothes. One day we managed to get our hands on a tube of lipstick, and June and I had a great time putting it on but it took a lot of getting off, and I had to tell a white lie about red cough sweets.

"I want you to help me this afternoon. Have you forgotten that Grandma and Grandad Burns are coming for tea? While you've got your coat on, you'd better nip round to the hardware shop and see if you can get some green soap. We've only a little bit left."

She looks up at the clock: "*Run*, Dorothy. They might be closing."

Taking her purse from her apron pocket, she pushes money into my hand and sinks back on to the settee. I dash up the road with mixed feelings — sad to have lost my afternoon with June, but pleased that my grandma and grandad are coming. We don't see them very often. They live in London. Mother is always writing to ask them to come and live near us; according to the news, London seems to be bombed almost every night and she is worried that they will be killed. But Grandma runs a fish and chip shop and she always writes the same thing in her letters: "I can't leave my shop, or the people of Whitechapel will starve to death." Mother doesn't believe that there are any people left in Whitechapel to feed, but Grandma and Grandad Burns won't leave.

The Post Office door is locked. I walk across the front of the Post Office and try the door to the hardware shop. It opens, but the lights are off and the shop is almost in darkness. I walk over to the counter and there, standing on a shelf behind the counter, is the block of soap I have come to buy. I am just going to call out for attention, when I hear:

"You lika that?"

Startled, I look around. There is no one in the shop. The curtain that hangs behind the counter, and which separates the living quarters from the shop, moves gently and a woman's voice sighs, softly:

"Frederico, don't. We shouldn't."

"You don't like I should do that?"

There is a moment's silence.

"I like."

The curtain moves again, and then starts to move quite violently.

"You'll push me into the shop."

"Then we go upstairs?"

There is a rustle of the curtain and the woman murmurs:

"Let me check the shop door."

196

I am standing in the middle of the shop. I should not be here. The curtain sways, and without a second thought, I drop behind boxes at the side of the counter. It takes some time for the woman to come from behind the curtain. Her feet are bare and with one hand she holds her blouse closed. She skips across the shop.

"It's open!" she calls.

With a click, the catch drops, with an unnerving grind, the bolt slides across and with a swish, the blind lowers. In the tiny bit of light that comes from behind the half-open curtain, I see a man walk into the shop. He isn't wearing a shirt and his hair is ruffled. I recognise him as the Italian prisoner of war. I see the woman's pale figure run back to him. Picking her off the floor, he swings her around, and they speak softly into each other's faces. As he kisses her, he holds her to him and she folds herself into his body.

"I take you on the boxes," he says.

She jerks away from him and slides to her feet.

"No, no, not here. Let's make it last."

He swings her up in his arms and they disappear through the curtain. I can hear them talking and laughing as I crouch behind the boxes. What have I just seen? I sit down heavily. My legs ache. My thoughts are leaping around everywhere, like hot flames through coals. That was a prisoner of war with the woman who has come to work in our Post Office. What did "take her" mean? Was she going to be taken away? I look around, and now I remember where I am, locked in the shop. I listen again. Silence. I run to the door, turn the lock and pull. It doesn't open. I pull again with all my might, shaking and rattling the door as I do so.

"Hello? Hello? We are closed," calls the woman.

The man's voice says:

"They go away. The door is locked. Come."

I crouch by the door and wait. Now shaking with fear, I stand and review the door. The bottom bolt is drawn across, so pulling myself together, I take hold of it and pull sideways. After what seems to be an eternity, the bolt slides across. I wait and listen. I rise to my feet and with care turn the lock. This time the door opens, and I slide through the small crack and run.

It is now raining hard. My hair and clothes are soaking. As I throw open the kitchen door, Mother comes through the green curtain.

"Is that you, Dorothy?"

"Yes, Mother," I reply.

"Where have you been all this time?"

Now I remember! I don't have the soap and I don't have the money either. The money is on the shop counter. I put it there before the curtain started to move.

"The Post Office was closed," I say, truthfully. Then I lie. "I tried some other shops, but they were all closed."

"Hum," she says. "Give me the money, then. We'll manage with the soap we've got."

She holds out her hand, waiting for the pennies to fall into it. Nothing happens.

"I've lost it."

For a moment there is silence.

"*Lost* it? Where have you *lost* it?"

"I don't know," I lie.

With a swipe she knocks me across the kitchen.

"Lost it? Lost it, my foot. I don't know what you've been up to, young lady, but whatever it was, it wasn't looking for soap. It's time someone took to you. Your father's not interested: you could turn into a scruffy know-nothing for all he is bothered."

She marches back through the curtain and returns with the large, black kettle. Steam rises around her as she stands over the sink. I stand behind her, my hair and jumper still wet. Pushing the empty kettle under the running tap, she turns to me.

"You may have your father wrapped around your finger, but you don't fool me. I've got your measure. Get those pots washed properly; see if you can earn the money you have lost."

I push the hair out of my face, pull my cold, damp jumper up from my shoulders and roll up the sleeves.

"And take that off before you stretch the sleeves."

I raise my arms and she peels off the jumper. As my face appears below it, she looks at me hard.

"I don't know what I'm going to do with you. You're more trouble than both the boys put together."

"Sorry," I murmur.

Sorry for what I am not sure. I turn to the bowl of steaming water. I can just see over its rim, but now I smile. Here I am safe. I know what to do and nothing will harm me, but as I wash the pots and pans piled before me, images and thoughts still run through my head. She had kissed him back. She had gone with him. She had not tried to escape. But as I get stuck into the soapy suds and the water warms me, I decide that she knew what she was doing and not to say a word to anyone.

Grandma and Grandad Burns come to tea. They bring us all presents and I get a tiny china doll that lives in a walnut shell.

"My goodness, look at the two of you! All grown up, hey?" says Grandma Burns as Jack, Bob and I stand before her. "Changed a bit since I last saw them, Nellie. Blimey, doesn't time fly? And look at this lovely boy — well, well, well. I've only heard talk about you. Pleased to meet you, Master Bob."

Grandma puffs and blows as she lowers herself into Father's chair and pulls Bob on to her lap. Father stands by the door and leans on the doorpost. I can't remember seeing Grandma Burns before, and I can't really understand much of what she says. She talks in a funny way, as if her tongue has got stuck in the front of her mouth. Grandad, who is small and bald-headed, smells of tobacco. He doesn't really speak much. He is somewhere a long way off, in a world of his own. He is a scientist, an inventor or an amateur, as Mother calls him. I have never seen his inventions but Mother told me that he had made a crystal set, what he called a cat's-whisker radio. When she was a girl she wore headphones and when Grandad moved the wires across the walls of the room she could hear people talking from all around the world. He is telling us now that since the war started the police have been to look at his radio once or twice, but as Grandma says, they all know him and he has always done mad things.

We have clear chicken soup and some of the bread that Mother has just baked. Father and Grandad have pressed beef and we all eat Mother's caraway seed cake. Grandad produces a bottle of whisky from his pocket, and with a good deal of ceremony he and Father take the small glasses from the china cabinet, and the bottle is soon empty.

Grandma and Grandad leave soon after we have eaten, as they have to catch the bus to Derby. They are staying the night with my mother's sister, Auntie Elsie. Mother tries to persuade Grandma to stay near us for a few days, but she won't.

"London will fall down if I don't go back. It's been bashed about enough with all the bombs. What will poor old London do if all the Londoners leave her?"

She smiles broadly and winks at me as she says this. I know that nothing will keep her from her old London. I wonder what London looks like and why she loves it so much. I have seen Sheffield once but I didn't think much of it.

It is very dark when they leave. Father walks with them down to the bus stop at the falling ends. It has taken a long time for Mother and Grandma to say goodbye, and now as Mother stands by the sink, tears are sliding down her face as fast as the water runs from the taps.

Later, as Mother sits on the settee listening to the wireless, I hang around doing nothing in particular.

"What's the matter with you?" she asks.

"Nothing," I reply.

She stops knitting and watches me.

"Mother, will Grandma and Grandad Burns ever come and see us again?"

"Maybe they will, some day — when the war is over."

Her eyes return to her knitting.

"Mother, will I have to leave you when I grow up? I mean, will I ever be a lady and have to leave home?"

She puts her head back and looks at me.

"Well, you might leave home, that's for sure. But what do you want to be a lady for? It's hard enough being a woman, never mind bothering with being a lady. I hope you leave home, Dorothy; there's not much in our village to stay for. What's this about anyway?"

"Well, my aunts are always saying I won't make a lady. June and her mother like to wear make-up. But I don't — it makes my face feel all stiff and funny."

She stops me.

"What do your aunts know about being a lady? They get it mixed up with being a snob. You'll be a lady."

She reaches over and takes my hand.

"Don't go rushing to grow up. Enjoy what you have. Let the other girls have the men and the babies, Dorothy. You use your brains, make something of yourself. It's a load of old baloney is love: it gets worn away by hard work and then it's the end of life."

I can forget the hands on legs and the lipstick. I will read books and do sums. I can understand these things.

We smile at each other in silent agreement.

CHAPTER
FOURTEEN

A few return, too few

March — May 1945

I am home from school. It is Friday afternoon: the week has ended and school can be forgotten for a couple of days. Something isn't quite right. The kitchen is cold, the bath is not there. Father is sitting in his chair, smoking his pipe. I look at him again and am surprised to see that he is wearing his Saturday clothes and doesn't have his old blanket covering the chair. Come to think of it, there is no fire and the kettle is singing, hot water still in it.

"Has something happened to Father?" I whisper.

Mother bursts out laughing.

"Your daughter wants to know if you are well or if something has happened to you."

"Come here, Dolly." Father laughs loudly and holds his arms out to me.

"We have pithead baths, Dolly! No more dirty clothes at home, no more baths in the kitchen. We have a hot shower when we finish work and we leave our dirty clothes in a locker."

His smile spreads from ear to ear, and now I can see that his very short hair has more gold in it than I have seen there recently. For a moment I feel almost sad. I will miss his panda eyes, with their bright blue centres, his large pink smile, his clumpy metal boots — but then I see Mother. She is standing by the curtain and she looks happy.

"And there will be no more awful, smelly, dirty clothes hanging around the house."

I am sitting on the chair arm. He looks like a different man, his hair all bristly clean and no black eyelashes.

"Did you get your baths at your Union meetings, the ones you went to in your best suit?"

"We did indeed. You wouldn't think a bar of soap and a drop of hot water would take so much arguing for. You and Bob could manage without them, couldn't you?"

"Uncle Arthur said that you wouldn't get anything. He said that the Union was a waste of time."

Mother grunts and disappears back into the kitchen.

"There are a few like him, Dolly. They don't believe in anything but themselves. It's selfo besto, damn and bugger resto. Some people seem to think that we have rights to nothing, Dolly. But I think we'll manage to teach them. Some of these young chaps who've come from other parts aren't just going to take it lying down."

He nods his head and sucks his pipe. Nothing happens. He looks into the bowl and frowns; then he puts the pipe on the mantelpiece and talks into the fire.

"The worst thing is when a working man thinks he can get what he wants just by shouting and yelling. Remember, Dolly, it's as I told you: don't try to climb up alone — that's what bullies do. They have to make a lot of effort, and it must be lonely living with self-pride for a friend. Take other people with you and learn to go with them. It'll be a big job but it will give people confidence and trust in each other. The last few years have taught us some hard lessons. We've just got to hang on to what we've learnt."

He picks up the poker and hits the top of the fire with it; silently he watches the poker heat up in the red coals. Only the muscles of his jaw are moving. I watch his face in silence and almost fall off the chair arm when, with a beaming smile, he swings back to me.

"I saw your Uncle Arthur taking a shower. He didn't think that was a waste of time. He was mucking in with the workers under that hot water, I can tell you."

Now he is laughing again and I laugh with him.

All day April rain has fallen: no hint of a shower, just driving wind and rain. My hair is wet and stuck to my forehead, and my feet are cold after the journey from school. I slam the kitchen door and wait for Mother to chastise my behaviour. But although I can see her standing by the table in the next room, she is silent. Divesting myself of my wet coat, I pass through the half-closed curtain, but still she remains by the table, the local newspaper spread out before her. Her hand grasps my sleeve and pulling me towards her, she says:

"Look at this, Dot."

I glance over Mother's shoulder.

"'Local man returns with Distinguished Service Medal'," I mumble.

"Read it! Read it!" Mother pushes the paper into my face. "It's Grace's husband! You know, the man who has the clothes shop across the road."

It takes a moment for the words to sink in, but I read on. "Lieutenant Charles Wentworth has returned home with severe injuries after serving behind enemy lines and has been recognised for his military distinction."

As the evening wears on, I try to imagine what "behind enemy lines" means. How did he get there? I drop on to Father's chair arm.

"Hello, Dolly," he says. "What's brought this honour my way?" He moves his paper to one side. I can no longer balance so easily beside him and as we sit we are almost at eye level. In a flash I know that my journeys to this resting place will be fewer.

"I wanted to ask you something."

"Um?" he says, his eyes back on his paper.

"Well, I was reading about the man from the clothes shop."

He stops me with a sharp look.

"You mean Lieutenant Wentworth? Let's have some respect here, Dorothy. What did you want to know?"

Now I feel silly, but there is nothing to do but press on.

"Well, I wondered how he got behind enemy lines."

"I don't know, Dorothy," says Father, "but a lot of our men were parachuted out behind enemy lines before the real fighting started. They were usually there to cause as much damage as possible. He was an engineer and worked on the railways. I don't know any more and it's not for us to know. All we need to know now is that he was a brave man."

A little party is arranged in his honour. Bunting goes up around the shop and we wait for Grace and her honoured husband to return. When Lieutenant Wentworth gets out of the car, I see that his right coat sleeve is pinned to his shoulder. As we enter the shop, the smell of new clothes invades me and I try to hide behind one of the racks. But now I am too tall.

Grace comes to find me. Our eyes meet — hers are less colourful and her cheeks are a little hollow — and she smiles at me.

"Hello, Miss Dorothy," she says, bending towards me. "The room is still yours, if you want it." Turning to her husband's call, she puts her hand on my head — and gives me a sweet.

We go to the picture house with Father on Friday evening. It is so noisy — everyone standing and cheering and clapping as the film shows the English and American soldiers marching into Berlin, and our allies the Russians coming in through war-ravaged streets.

All day on Saturday and Sunday the wireless is on, but there is still no news of the war's end and no news of where Hitler has gone. We are outside in the garden a lot; everyone is talking all the time, drinking tea and waiting. Every time the wireless commentator's voice comes on, there are loud shushings and people run for their doors.

But by the end of the weekend they are still playing music. On Sunday evening Father has to go to work. We go to bed reluctantly, praying that the next day will bring the news we are all waiting to hear.

Crash! The stair-foot door bangs against the wall. I am sitting up in bed.

"Nellie! It's over! We've bloody done it! We've won!"

Father's feet pound the stairs. Mother has just swung her legs out of bed, and still carrying his snap tin and water bottle, Father lifts her and swings her around. I can't remember seeing my parents kiss before, but they do now.

Jack and Bob fly into the bedroom, jumping and leaping about. We go downstairs and Father is talking faster than I have ever heard.

"They signed the surrender early this morning. The pit manager heard it. We all came up early."

He turns on the wireless. The commentator is saying the same as Father. The National Anthem is played and we dance to it. Eventually, we go back up to bed.

In the morning, the birds sing out and the gardens are full of voices. Church bells ring in the distance. Outside our house, an elderly lady calls out:

"Three cheers for today! Hip, hip, hooray! Hip, hip, hooray! Hip, hip, hooray!"

The gate bursts open, and Bert and Arthur fall through it.

208

"Goodness, you are early. Where is your mother?" asks our mother.

"She's in the house," says Arthur.

"Did the bells get her up?" Mother is closing the gate.

"No, she's been up all night, listening to the wireless," Bert replies.

Arthur turns back to the gate. "She wouldn't go to bed. She said she had to wait up for Dad to come home now that it is over."

As he turns back, tears are running down his face.

"We told her he can't come back, as he's dead, but she says that she hasn't seen him dead, so she won't believe it," says Bert.

Mother gives us all bread and jam and cups of tea. Father hugs the twins and Mother is on her way out to visit Mrs Baker.

We run down the road. Cars pass, horns blaring. The people in the paper shop have put some Union Jacks across the front and the street is full. People seem to be walking around in circles — no one seems to know quite what to do. At the falling ends the chemist has hung flags over his doorway. The bells have gone quiet and Constable White, standing next to his bicycle, his usually stern face beaming, says the ringers probably had to stop because their arms ache and they've had no practice for so long.

Some young men are trying to put a flag on the traffic lights. One jumps down and I am shocked when I realise that it is Harry.

"Where's George?" Jack asks.

"He's gone to call for Mike," says Harry, but before we can turn George has jumped on Jack's back and Mike is standing there with his jumper sticking out.

Mrs Meeks's voice rings out. We all jump to attention, but the orders are not for us. She is instructing the caretaker, who is hanging the school's Christmas decorations across the front of the school. End of the war or not, he never misses a chance to give us a warning.

"Be careful, you lot. Don't go breaking those windows."

Flags have appeared outside houses. On a wall by the old mill are two huge posters. One is of Churchill with his fingers in the V for Victory sign and the other is of Stalin, the Russian leader, with "Guns for Joe" written on it. I wonder who could have got them up there.

Father is busy lifting a branch of a tree up on to the top of other branches. "Bonfire tomorrow," he announces before the questions can come.

Now we are down the gitty. Lieutenant Wentworth is standing by his shop, a stepladder unopened by his feet, a hammer in his one hand. Dodging a car, Harry is across the road.

"Shall I put those up for you, sir?" Harry is almost as tall as Lieutenant Wentworth and with the help of the rest of us, the clothes shop front is soon decorated with coloured paper streamers. His wife comes out of the shop, pulling on her coat — her hair is not as high as once it had seemed to be, and nor are her lips so red. Placing her arm around my shoulders, she asks:

"Where is your mother?"

210

I smile. I am too happy to be worried by her today.

As she speaks, Mother appears. Kissing the top of my head, which is now at shoulder level, the lady at the shop whispers:

"Never would sell you, would she?"

Out of habit we walk across to Bert and Arthur's house. We sit and stand by our steps, now too big to all fit on them. Grandma walks down her path, on the arm of Auntie Betty. She looks pale and tired, but she hasn't received any telegrams yet and now I think she may never.

Mike appears. "Would anyone like a piece of bread?"

He holds a newspaper high above his head. With a whoop and a yell we descend on him. A thousand crumbs explode in the air and fall to the ground. We scrabble around to retrieve what we can. Mike's jam sandwiches are the best in the world.

I look in through the window of the twins' house. I can make out Mrs Baker. She is sitting on a chair in the living room. I leave the boys and go in.

"Hello, Mrs Baker."

My call is loud and exaggerated but she does not answer. She does not move. She is alone, inside herself, and she just sits and looks down at her hands. I unlock the front door and let Mother in. I wait patiently as Mother persuades Mrs Baker to leave the house.

I dance down to the crossroads. Mother and Mrs Baker follow, walking slowly, arm in arm. We dance in the streets for the entire day; the whole village — those who remain — is out celebrating. The procession around the green is continuous, the May sun shining on our faces.

By sundown I am tired and my legs ache, and as I walk down the hill from the Post Office I hear my father's voice calling to me.

"You want a ride, Dolly?"

Without waiting for an answer he swings me into the air and places me on his shoulders. Now I am going down the hill, riding on Father's back. Mr Churchill's face looks down from on high. Uncle Arthur falls into step next to us.

"We've done it then, Joe. We've beat the buggers."

Father looks sideways at his brother.

"Yes, we've beaten them in Germany, Arthur."

He looks back at the face of Churchill.

"But now we've got to fight this lot at home and they are going to take some beating. We've got to vote them out."

The bonfire burns and we dance on into the night. Baked potatoes, hot from the embers, burn our hands; beer, newly released from pub cellars, wets our whistles, old and young. For tonight we are united as one, and our celebrations are loud and joyful.

But when morning comes the bonfire is dead and the road is empty and silent. Father is at the pit, Mother is arm-deep in the washing and my brothers have run on to school. The excitement of last night is gone, and while I know the world has shifted and we are the winners, I am still walking to school in my worn-out shoes.